Not a Bad Trip
A
Pittsburgh
Cab Story

HOWIE EHRLICHMAN

WORD ASSOCIATION PUBLISHERS
www.wordassociation.com
1.800.827.7903

ISBN: 978-1-63385-500-7
Library of Congress Control Number: 2023914492

Published by
Word Association Publishers
205 Fifth Avenue
Tarentum, Pennsylvania 15084

www.wordassociation.com
1.800.827.7903

Contents

Introduction

Oh, where- you going to, my lady blue?
It's a shame you ruined your gown in the rain.
She just looked out the window, she said,
Sixteen Parkside Lane

– From **Taxi**, *by Harry Chapin*

Sixteen Parkside Lane could stand as an intriguing title for a book; just saying. As you may have guessed by my selection of cited lyrics, I am an admirer of the late, great Harry Chapin. A revered humanitarian and thoughtful poet, Harry was music's eminent storyteller. And of all the incredible songs in his portfolio, his *Taxi* story was peerless. While I could never write a taxi story with such a level of elegance, have a godawful singing voice, can't read music, or even play a rudimentary instrument, I have one tool in the shed: a treasure trove of cab experience.

I wish I kept a copy of a 1970*ish* Pittsburgh Post Gazette featuring a column with the byline, *A Write Guy* above a picture of yours truly. Each Saturday, the newspaper chose one of its carriers to be honored as *Paperboy of the Week*. After Mr. Mazefsky, my route manager, nominated me, a reporter called for a brief interview. Inevitably, the *"what do you want to be when you grow up"* question surfaced. I was dumbfounded. My early childhood premonition of a bus driver was in temporary remission—I had to think of *something*. My sixth- grade teacher, Miss Hershey, once said I should be a writer, so I blurted out that answer. And fifty years later, I finally fulfilled that promise and finished my first book.

When initially bit by the creative bug, I enrolled in an adult education writing course at Community College to shake off the rust. It was "a little" embarrassing on day one to have the entire class turn in my direction with varying degrees of *WTF* expressions while the instructor discussed genres and I asked, "what's a genre?" I knew then I had a long way to go.

The inspiration for this project was twofold. Passengers often pressed their cab driver du-jour to recount their "craziest cab stories." And, I had recently read *Waiter Rant*, Steve Dublanica's hilarious and eye-opening account of the restaurant business from a server's perspective. I wondered if a marketplace existed in the literary world for a similar book told from a cab driver's point of view, and if so, would I be the right person to write it?

As I did my research, I was surprised and delighted to learn of several books on the market penned by cabbies and ex-cabbies. If you enjoy *Not a Bad Trip: A Cab Story,* two of my favorites were *Hack,* by Dmitry Samarov and *Confessions of a New York Taxi Driver* by Eugene Salomon. Mr. Samarov's writing chronicled a ten- year stint cabbing in Chicago, along with his artistic sketches, while Mr. Salomon's work offered a plethora of taxi tales from thirty-five years in the front seat of a New York City cab.

Although most taxi memoirs I found were set in the largest metropolitan areas, like Chicago, New York, or Toronto, I concluded there may be a niche for stories from a smaller city, maybe even my big-small town. While I began my cab adventures in the same year as Eugene Salomon (1977), I realized my experiences paled compared to his multiple decades of full- time cabbing. Yet, I had my own stories to tell. Even though my service to Pittsburgh's taxicab world was not uninterrupted, over a forty- year period between the first and final chapters, I accrued a good twenty-three years behind the wheel. And that included a minimum of three years in each of five decades from the seventies thru the twenty-tens...or was it the twenty-teens? Plus, my "real job" careers in the food business and public transit only enriched my perspective as a seasoned, been there done that, cabby. I knew I had to write this book.

If time travel was a thing, I would beam—or whatever—back to my cabbing days, purchase a hundred spiral notepads from a back-to-school sale, and commit to chronicle at least a single moment in time from each day behind the wheel. A casual observation, a notable conversation, or the newest thing the world taught me that day would suffice. Unfortunately, moving through time is not (yet?) an option, but what I have always had is a remarkable long-term memory. I can still recount vivid, minute details from the earliest parts of life, some important, many so trivial that no one else would ever try to remember. Just don't ask me about where I was or what happened an hour ago. So, welcome to my back seat, buckle up—if the seatbelt still works—and enjoy the ride.

Chief – A Prologue

September 2013

The Mobile Data Terminal overflows with pending fares on a summery Pittsburgh evening. Many of these trips are heading to weekend city hot spots, South Side being the most popular. Blessed with an endless stretch of bars, clubs, and restaurants lining East Carson, its main street, South Side is the go- to place in *the 'burgh* for partying, people watching, and rabble rousing.

I punch into zone 308, with its long queue of awaiting fares. The dispatch screen buzzes with *Fare Waiting* printed boldly upon it. I hit the *Accept* key, and within seconds, an address appears. Looks much the same as my previous five trips—Friday night revelers eager to join the in-crowd. I call the provided cell phone number, informing my newest client,

Megan, that her taxi is only two minutes away. The young lady sounds enthusiastic and says they are ready to roll.

Two minutes later, I pull in front of a well- preserved, brownstone apartment building in the fashionable Shadyside neighborhood, seeing no sign of life—or at least of anyone looking for a ride. I press the computer's *Call Out* button to reinforce my presence. "Which part of *two minutes* is so hard to figure out?" I wonder out loud as I await a response. Finally, the screen flashes another message—*Coming Out in Five Minutes*.

Wonderful! I continue to wait, albeit with growing impatience. Time is money. After a mini-eternity, several human-like figures emerge from the building. These must be the folks who claimed to be ready ten minutes ago.

A group of four, two guys and two girls, in their late twenties, make their way to the taxi. They appear not to be coupled, likely some friends seeking adult- beverages and companionship. The men lamely attempt to conceal large, red, liquid- filled plastic cups, as both passenger side doors simultaneously open.

"What's up there…Chief?" the young man staking claim on the front seat inquires.

I close my eyes, imagining an impressive bouquet of feathers upon my head. "Hey, what's up— by the way, you need to lose the beers."

Both women slide across the back seat, skillfully manipulating their miniscule black dresses from providing maximum exposure. The second guy, beverage in hand, flashes a look as if I had just assaulted his emotional well-being. "Don't worry; you'll get a bigger tip if you let us drink in your cab."

My patience thins. "Sorry dude, not worth a fine or my license—open containers ain't cool in the cab. Chug 'em or dump 'em."

One chugs, one dumps, everyone's finally in. The shotgun passenger, I secretly nickname *Stiffler*, as he instantly reminds me of a character from the movie *American Pie*. Every group of friends in this generation seems to have their own version of Stiffler—that classic, yet still strangely likeable, douchebag.

The women introduce themselves. "Hi, Mr. Cab Driver! I'm Kelly and this is Megan, we're gonna, like, party!" I glance in the rearview mirror, acknowledging the young ladies. The interior of the cab is dark, but it's hard not to notice both are quite attractive.

I force a smile, "Hey, I'm Howie," while wondering *what they are doing with these two bozos?* as we join the Fifth Avenue traffic.

"Take us to the *Sous-side...*Chief!" commands Stiffler's back seat buddy.

Now I envision myself wearing a fire battalion commander's helmet.

The trip begins with many of the requisite, standardized cab driver questions. I wonder why people develop investigative journalistic instincts whenever they enter a taxi with their peers. *Is it a busy night? Do you go to the South Side a lot? Is this the Cash Cab? How long have you been driving a cab?* The same old, routine curiosities I hear any given weekend.

"How long have you been driving a cab?" should be so simple to answer. For me, it is rather complex. I usually say something like *for a really, long time*; or *longer than I can remember*. Or be a smart-ass and say, *since about four o'clock*.

3

For this group, I offer this half-truth— "Oh, for about thirty-five years." This is, oddly, both true and false, but it works for this moment.

"Wow!" exclaims Megan. "Like, you've been doing this, like… forever, and you don't even look that…old."

Stiffler's backseat buddy joins in. "Man, you must have some stories to tell. How many people have had sex in your cab?"

Before I can respond, not that I really want to, Stiffler raises that inevitable, hey, watch me relate to the cabby to impress my friends, question— "What's the craziest thing that has ever happened to you?"

I hear that a dozen times every weekend when chauffeuring the party crowd. Yes, crazy things absolutely do happen in cabs. There are so many wild stories, however, repeating them over and over gets old. Besides, they are paying me for a ride, not an oral presentation. I white lie, "Man, there's so many. I just can't think of anything specific off the top of my head."

Not the reply they wanted. Kelly, seated directly behind me, lightly touches my shoulder. "Come on, Howie, you know you want to, like, tell *me* a wild taxi-story."

We swing onto the Birmingham Bridge toward South Side. "No, really. Nothing exciting happens—nothing that stands out."

Stiffler's buddy rejoins the fray. "Come on, Chief. You can tell us. Don't you want to tell your story?"

My annoyance rises as we merge into the Carson Street congestion. "I guess I'm just not a great storyteller," I chuckle, "but really, I've seen enough on this job that I could probably write a book." A gigantic light bulb suddenly supplants my imaginary fire and tribal chiefs.

Stiffler shoots me a look that screams, *if you could write a book, you wouldn't be driving a taxi!* Nonetheless, he switches gears, allowing a more amicable side of his personality to check the impending douche-baggage. "Hey, I'd be first in line to buy that book!"

Our journey ends as we pull over at 20th and East Carson. The meter flashes $10.65. Stiffler's buddy hands me a crisp twenty-dollar bill. "That's all you!"

"Hey, thanks guys. You all have a great evening!"

"Howie, you'd better write that book!" Megan insists, struggling unsuccessfully to keep the hemline of her tiny black dress from providing a momentary, cheap thrill as she slides across the back seat. Stiffler gives an unsubtle nod of approval.

"Check your local bookstore in a few years, I'll promise to dedicate a chapter to you guys!" I manage a sincere smile.

Megan, now out of the cab, leans in and beams, "That would be, like, so awesome!" The doors shut as the foursome blended into the South Side show.

I glance at the hard-earned twenty and file it neatly in my wallet.

Signal four

June 1977

My heart races as I slow-walk through the open gate housing Yellow Cab's East Liberty Garage. The spacious yard appears half-filled with scattered Checker taxicabs, a few looking new, coated with fresh, canary-yellow paint, most faded and well-worn, others ready for the junkyard. I take a deep breath as I make my way into the building, remembering my instructions to find the man locked inside a cage.

The facility is a two-story, brick warehouse with offices on the second floor, including the exchange—the radio dispatchers' and call-takers' workshop. The lower level contains the cashier-garage dispatch office, commonly called the "the cage." Several bays and work- stations for the mechanics and technicians occupy the rest of the concrete floor.

An office with bullet-proof windows and steel doors, the cage is where the cashiers dispatch and check in cabs. Tightly secured offices are typical in taxi garages, designed to protect the high amount of currency exchanged, perhaps also to shield the dispatchers from crazed cab drivers. A small slot on the bottom of the window allows enough room for cash and paperwork to be transacted.

Several drivers line up at the cage, some waiting to begin work, others sacrificing their daily tithes to the taxi-gods. A couple guys eyeball me, probably thinking, "Here comes another sucker—wonder how long he'll last?"

As my turn finally arrives, I slide my newly minted piece of cardboard— *County of Allegheny Chauffeur's License*— through the window. Fred, the cashier, examines it, nods, then produces a yellow blank trip manifest and a single key. On the manifest, he etches *125* on the line marked cab number and *505* in the driver's number space.

I wander aimlessly around the maze of yellow Checkers until spotting the one numbered 125, a battle-scarred vehicle having seen its best days long ago. Opening the creaky, driver's side door, and sinking into the generic gray, weathered front bench seat, I can barely see over the steering wheel or touch the pedals. I reach down for the seat adjustment and yank it as close to the front as possible. Not especially comfortable; but workable.

I study the folded accordion, cardboard information packet received during my single day of training, which includes locations of various taxi-stands or posts, radio procedures, and taxi driving tips, while cranking open both front windows. Circa 1977, power- windows and air-conditioning are rare luxuries. The only radio is the two-way with Yellow

Cab Dispatch. I will sorely miss blasting my favorite tunes. I fire the cab up; showtime—ready to roll!

I drive to a nearby taxi-stand. Several calls come over the radio, some close by. I hesitate while the trips are quickly scooped up by other cabs. After a good hour, I finally get a fare. I cannot recall any details of my first four trips, except for the fourth, which landed me at the border of Wilkinsburg, a community abutting the East End of Pittsburgh.

Once again, I consult the cardboard cab bible to discover *Wilkinsburg 3* is the closest call post. I locate a rusted Taxi-Cab Stand sign on West Street and park. Is this a good spot on a slow Tuesday night? Not likely. Another glance at my handy Yellow Cab packet shows other options for an open call. I'm near Homewood, a neighborhood known for its crime rate, perhaps a place to avoid on my first night. Squirrel Hill, an area I know well, is within range—a definite comfort zone.

"Edgewood One, Edgewood... " the radio blares, "Edgewood open!"

Hey, I think I'm close to Edge...

Does not matter, as a quicker competitor pounces on the call. The dispatcher offers a few other trips that I freeze on while they are rapidly gobbled up by the competition. As he does every fifteen minutes, the dispatcher announces the time— *KGD-225, Yellow Cab Time; 9:30PM.* This is frustrating, much harder than I ever imagined. After five hours, my only fares are the four mediocre trips scribbled on my manifest.

"Squirrel Hill 4, *Squirrel 4.*" cackles the anonymous voice as I grab and prepare to key the microphone. "Squirrel Hill 4, open!"

"One-two-five, One-two-five!" I bellow into the mic.

"Ok, One -two-five cab, Poli's, 2607 Murray, for James."

"Poli's for James!" I repeat enthusiastically.

I begin feeling better. I had never dined at Poli's, a popular seafood restaurant close to my home, but knew Larry, the owner's son, as I used to deliver his newspaper route when his family took their summer vacations. Now, I'm rolling there for a cab trip; this is kind of cool!

A Black, thirty-something couple motion to my beat- up cab. As they make their way into the ample back seat, the gentleman requests, "Take us to Federal Street on the North Side."

We turn left on Forward Avenue to enter the Parkway towards Downtown. Finally, a decent trip! The lady asks if we could divert and add an extra stop along the way. They directed me to an apartment building in Uptown, went inside for a minute, returned, and we were rolling again.

"So," the gentleman inquires, "How long have you been driving a taxi, my man?"

Laughing, I reply, "Uh, for about five hours. This is my first day on the job."

Ten minutes later, we arrived at our destination. I know little about North Side, except for the main streets and hospitals but realize the area surrounding North Avenue and Federal are not among the swankiest parts of town. The man exits while his female counterpart stays in the cab, engaging me with pleasant small talk. Several minutes later, the man returns, asking if we could make yet another stop before taking them home.

"Sure, no problem!" I beam. The meter clicks past $14.00… not a bad trip!

"Next, we need to stop in the South Side," directs the gentleman, reciting a set of cross streets. This is fantastic! We had already crossed one river, now we get to cross two more! For a native Pittsburgher, crossing a river is like entering another world.

We pull over in the East Carson Street business district and they both exit. "We'll be back in ten minutes, my man," the man promises. I glance again at the meter, ticking away a dime at a time, eclipsing $20, and going strong. Not only am I making money for myself, but for Yellow Cab too. I think they will be impressed with my productivity on the first day on the job! *Ok, give me a break—I'm nineteen years old…I know everything!*

The couple returns, directing me to their next destination. We climb a series of steep, sloping, narrow, winding roads. I have little familiarity with this part of the city; we are light years away from my comfort zones.

After a series of twists and turns through a dark, heavily wooded area, we turn left. Fisher Street springs to life with people, mostly young and African American. As we wind through this endless complex of worn, red-brick buildings, I try appearing nonchalant as the bright yellow taxicab dissects the neighborhood, attracting undivided attention. "Ok, my man, please stop right past this dumpster." The polite gentleman kisses his companion goodbye and leaves the vehicle.

"Driver, I have just one more stop to make, then you can take me home," orders the woman.

The street encircles in the shape of a gigantic horseshoe. Groups of people eyeball us as we meander through the projects. About three-fourths of the way through, I exhale a sigh of relief as the main road leading out of this place comes into view.

"Ok driver, turn left here," the passenger requests. Not at all what I wanted to hear at this point! I begrudgingly veer from the horseshoe onto another side street, close to the end of the complex. "Stop at that building right there; I gotta run in for a couple minutes and I'll be right back—don't worry; no one will bother you up here." The door shuts and I watch her disappear up steps between buildings.

I try to remain positive, although I now realize this all may not end happily ever after. The meter ticks to $27, more than all my previous trips combined. I hope she returns. They have been with me for well over an hour, making multiple stops, and returning to the cab every time—sure she will be back!

The passing minutes become an eternity. Small clusters of curious young people begin appearing in the rear- view mirror. Those couple of minutes stretch to ten. Was my great trip turning into a bad dream? Did she forget about me? *Uh-oh—I'm fucked!* Should I cut my losses and get out of here? I might get fired if I come up short on my first night on the job.

"Well," I rationalize, "what could happen if I get out and try to find out where she went? These kids will be cool with me if I just ask." *Silly me!*

Exiting the vehicle, trying to appear calm, cool, and collected, I approached a group of neighborhood teens who were making their way towards my taxi. "Hey, how are y'all doin'?

Do you happen to know where this lady"—I begin a brief, vague description— "lives?" Before I could elaborate, I find myself encircled by seven; five guys with two girls.

An imposing, hefty kid steps forward. "You got fucked, *mahfuckah!*" Within seconds, my 5' 8", 140- pound frame is pinned against the taxicab's left rear fender. A younger, wiry framed kid, knife in hand, scurries to the open driver's side door—at least I wasn't stupid enough to leave the key in the ignition. As my newfound acquaintance, who I entitle the imaginary nickname of *Fat Ass*, freezes me in place, I observe his accomplice attempting to slice the wire on the radio's mic—my only lifeline. One of the girls in the group approaches, then spits, her slobber landing on my shirt sleeve. Something—perhaps the humiliating hocker, injected me with the adrenaline to shove Fat Ass away with enough force for him to fall hard on the street, several feet away, as his cohorts looked on. I wrestle the smaller kid out of the cab, his pocket- knife dropping to the floor, near the brake pedal. Shaking, I fumble for the key, fire up the cab, and slam it into reverse. Fat Ass, meanwhile, is back on his feet, making a beeline for the taxi. Next thing I hear is a loud thud as I sideswipe my huge, threatening nemesis to the ground. I continue backing up, grasping desperately for the microphone, trying to catch my breath.

"One-two-five, emergency, one-two-five; signal four! One-two-five on a four!"

"Ok, one- twenty- five cab, location? Where are you?"

"I don't know where the fuck I am!" *(FCC Radio Violation #1)*

"Do you see a street sign... landmark?"

"I don't know—a bunch of apartment buildings…Boni-fay Street?" I finally notice a faded street sign.

"Help is on the way!"

Within two minutes, a Housing Authority Police car, lights flashing, races through the complex, as an unmarked white Pittsburgh Police unit, tailed by a black and white, roar in from the main road into the housing development. A crowd gathers as the excitement escalates, but my assailants have disappeared, including Fat Ass, despite his gracious brush with my taxi. As I explained my ordeal to the officers, small rocks rain down upon the streets, close to the police cars. "Let's get the hell out of here!" said one of the plain-clothes officers. "Follow us!"

They lead me out of the projects, onto a quieter side street, where the uniformed cops write down my information. As I rehash what had happened, the older of the two officers, a Mister Rogers look-alike, seems amazed by my naivety. When I mention that this is my first night driving a taxi, he smiles as he says, "At least yins cabbies learn quick—stay away from Saint Clair Village." They jot down a report number to give to the cab company. I thank them profusely for their rapid response. We shake hands and go our separate ways.

I return to Yellow Cab, manifest properly filled out with my other four trips. The cashier slides me an incident report to fill out and seems to be not the least bit impressed or surprised by my misadventure.

I walk out of the building, taking a breath of midnight air, feeling defeated, just a total loser. Will I be fired or held accountable for the uncollected fare? The commission earned from the other four trips would not even come close to paying for that lost revenue. I wonder how else this situation might have turned out. Did they want to rob me? Kill me? Humiliate me—or none of the above? I will never know for sure.

As I leave the taxi lot, sauntering along Centre Avenue, gazing at the idle parade of steel rear bumpers of yellow numbered Checker Marathons kissing the inside of a chain-linked fence, there was only one thing I did know for sure—I absolutely cannot wait to come back and try this again!

Saint Clair Village was vacated and demolished in 2010.

Yellow Cab Garage flanked by Instant Car Wash

CHAPTER 2

Basic Training

June 1977

The first day of school, the first date, the first day on the job. That first time. Those firsts become embedded within a person's subconscious. Decades later, that first night on the cab remains an enduring deposit in my memory bank. As you guessed, I went back and tried it again... and *again* and *again* and *again*. Why? Why not? Was it the money? The parade of intriguing people? A love of driving? Gambling instinct? Death wish? What could motivate a nineteen-year-old to undertake such a risky gig?

As a sophomore at Penn State's branch campus in nearby Mckeesport, I was confused and unsure of the future. I wanted to finish school, mostly for my parents, as I was the first person in my family to attend college. I was also gainfully employed at The Greengrocer, a local produce market, working there for almost three years, enjoying the job, while maintaining a respectable grade point average.

For junior year, I would be transferring to the main campus in State College, PA. Back then, it was feasible to work one's way through school. Knowing that I was leaving that fall, I realized the need to sock away some extra money over the summer. My dad had been driving a cab for several years, made a decent living, and liked his job. Originally hired as a delivery boy for the store, I had always enjoyed being on the road, so, why not drive a taxi part time over the summer?

Upon approaching my parents with this brilliant idea—I thought all of my ideas were beyond brilliant—they did not respond as I had expected. My father said I was too young and the job far too dangerous. They offered to help with my expenses, but I possessed this fierce trifecta of independence, rebellion, and stubbornness. The following morning, I headed to Yellow Cab and filled out an application.

I received a response from the cab company a few days later. After a short interview, I was hired, but kept it from my folks until the night before I was to report for training. They were less than thrilled, but reluctantly accepting of my newest adventure. I later learned that Dad told the garage supervisors to *keep an eye on me,* whatever that meant; I'm sure it was well intended.

Training day was not quite the vivid memory as some of those milestone firsts earlier alluded to. Our lessons began in a small conference room where we, a group of four, were fed an endless buffet of company policies and safety tips. We learned radio procedures, including six codes used to communicate with the dispatchers. Although we have not used them in years—all communications are now via a computerized system—I remember them well. *Signal One* was the call for a breakdown, *Signal Two* was to update traffic information, *Signal Three* was to report an accident, and *Signal Five* was for requesting directions or phoning a passenger. Hard as it is to imagine, cell phones were but a futuristic fantasy. My favorite signal was the *Six*, reporting a trip to the airport, fondly referred to as "The Promised Land." And, of course, there was the least favorite—that dreaded *Signal Four*, the 9-1-1 distress call.

After our classroom, we were introduced to the *school car*, cab#123, a pristine 1976 Checker Motors Taxi Edition, complete with jump seats, meter, and two-way radio. Bill, our instructor, was a seasoned taxi professional. We each took turns driving to the various stops along the way. I must admit that it was kind of a cool car to drive for the first time. As we drove past Three Rivers Stadium, we learned that Art Rooney, the legendary patriarch of the Pittsburgh Steelers, lived in the same house he grew up in on the North Side near the stadium. Instructor Bill explained how Mr. Rooney ritually called Yellow Cab every Sunday morning for a ride to church and faithfully tipped a quarter. Next, we headed north to our local union office, officially becoming proud members of Teamsters Local 128. We were lectured to look "presentable" and always wear a clean shirt with a collar.

The most memorable segment of our road training adventure was when one of the guys in our group asked Bill about strategies for taxi driving success as we approached Millvale, a small borough ten minutes northeast of Downtown. Bill's proclamation went something like this: "*Millvale*....hmmm....*Millvale*....well, if you're in *Millvale* or near *Millvale* and there's a call in *Millvale*, you might want to take the *Millvale* call, or you might not, but I would never sit in *Millvale* waiting for a *Millvale* call, or even chase out to *Millvale* for a *Millvale* call, cause nothing ever really happens in *Millvale*, but if you get a trip to *Millvale* or around *Millvale*..."

From Millvale, our next stop was the county courthouse in Pittsburgh, to be fingerprinted, photographed, and stripped of ten bucks each for our County of Allegheny Chauffeur's License.

During the ride back to Yellow Cab headquarters, I stared at my new license, tried to retain all that I had learned about the ins and outs of taxi-driving, and, of course, Millvale, and declared myself roadworthy.

Flag thrown; Meter on.

Millvale today is a happening place.

CHAPTER 3

The Checkered Past

I recovered from culture shock and returned for another shift two days after my Saint Clair Village welcome and wakeup call. The game plan for the summer was to keep my day job at Greengrocer and work a couple nights per week at Yellow Cab. While I could see the money-making potential in taxi driving, the lure of adventure, excitement and independence was an even greater draw.

Learning the tricks of the trade of the taxicab industry was not as easy as expected. My first impression of it being a matter of luck gradually unraveled. It took that entire summer and beyond to realize that successful cab driving was closer to 10% good or bad luck and 90% experience and strategy.

The best thing about this "just for summer" gig was the flexibility. Although an official employee of Yellow Cab Company—*Driver #505 at your service*—I was part time, unbound to any specific schedule. I could work around my job, school, social life, or whatever else happened to be on the agenda. To remain in good standing, the only requirement was to show up at least once per month.

Drivers were commission-based employees, receiving a generous 45% of all metered and flat-rated fares. In addition to our paychecks, there were, of course, tips, which were an even greater incentive—nothing more reinforcing than a pocketful of cash at the end of a night. I appreciated those weekly checks, even though they were diluted by union dues and taxes, including a 10% "tip tax."

Tip tax, familiar to many service industry workers, presumed specified percentages of gratuities as income. A simple example: A driver's one day total "book" —gross metered revenue—was $100. At 45%, his commission was $45; however, that income was taxed based on $55, assuming the driver collected an additional 10% ($10 on $100) in gratuities. This was never a problem, as most drivers exceeded well over 10% in actual tips. Tipping is both a fine art and an applied science, deserving so much more attention than can be accommodated in any single book, though it will be studied often throughout this one.

One thing I learned early was how it was worthwhile for drivers to tip the cage cashiers to get a decent cab—or even a crappy one—when the supply of available cabs was outstripped by the demand of the drivers. Although I was close to the bottom of the barrel, we were a union shop—a good thing—and seniority prevailed. Most full timers had steady (regularly assigned) cabs, with the rest prioritized based on status—full-timers over part-timers—and hire date. At times, even to this day, drivers without a steady cab may wait hours to be delegated a piece of equipment.

Yellow had two garages, the one in East Liberty, and in Manchester, on the city's North Side, each housing about half the fleet. Both employed full time staff, including cashiers, gas men—the folks who fueled and checked fluids in the cabs—and mechanics. The entire fleet of approximately 350 cabs consisted of the boxy Checker sedans, featuring their bulky, retro 1950's body style. With two retractable steel jump seats between the ample front and rear vinyl bench seats, they easily accommodated seven adults or eight children. Seat belts were seldom seen, let alone worn. Although the trunk contained a large tube radio, there was abundant space to haul a generous volume of luggage or cargo. The cabs' conditions varied greatly, even though they were rarely more than five years old. The difficult to navigate roadways, steep terrain, and brutal winters of Western Pennsylvania were never kind to cars; not even taxis built to endure such abuse.

While sparsely equipped, every cab had two essential tools of the trade: the meter and two-way radio. The meter was a sturdy, steel structure, with a large lever, known as "the flag." To activate the meter, the driver *threw the flag* one notch clockwise, enabling it to measure mileage through a connection to the rear wheels, along with a built- in timer to clock waiting time. When the taxi was vacant, the roof marquis reading "Yellow" automatically lit, with the flag's handle visible inside the windshield. Today, most meters are electronic, requiring only a push of a wimpy plastic button digitally displaying the fare. Call me nostalgic, but I miss throwing the heavy, metal flag and listening to the miles click into money.

The other important work-tool was the radio. Unlike Chicago or New York, Pittsburgh was never a cab town where you could stroll to any semi-main thoroughfare and easily hail a passing taxi. A significant percentage of our business consisted of the call and demand variety, and the cab's radio connected us with those trips.

The radio orders were organized geographically, utilizing two or three separate channels throughout the busiest hours, while broadcasting all fares on a single frequency during the quieter times. A common misconception was that the dispatchers systematically mandated the closest cabs to specific calls, but that was not the reality in Pittsburgh, or in most other markets. At Yellow, the fares aligned with the nearest cab stand or call post to the trip. The densest, busiest city neighborhoods had multiple posts, where dispatchers pinpointed each call within a few square blocks, while outlying boroughs and suburbs had only one or two, often encompassing several square miles of territory.

The protocol was simple, yet sophisticated. The call takers compiled the information, including the address, phone number, and name onto a formatted notecard, then fed it through an air powered conveyor belt to the dispatchers. The dispatcher determined which area, by call post, was the closest to the pending fare, and announced the post call twice. If a driver was—or claimed to be—parked at that cab stand, it was automatically their order. When there was no response to the initial call, after a brief pause, the trip was called "open" and awarded to the first three- digit cab number heard bidding for it. For example:

Dispatcher: *North Side 7, North Side 7.*

Radio Frequency: (crickets)

Dispatcher: *North Side 7, open!*

Radio Frequency: *Squelch...8...blurb...buzz...4...static... unintelligible...4-7-1...5...3-1-6...*

Dispatcher: *Okay, 471,471, Heinz 57, Main Gate for William.*

Radio Frequency: *4-7-1, Heinz for William.*

Dispatcher: *Roger, 471.*

In this case, there was strong competition for the open trip. The first full cab number coming through the noise was 4-7-1, who thus received the call. At busier times, many calls were not answered right away, remaining open, or "on the board." When these situations arose, the dispatchers broadcasted the awaiting calls, organized by their unique versions of alphabetical or geographic sequences, attempting to fill the orders. They often sounded like auctioneers as they rattled off the pending fares in their finest,distinctive Pittsburgh accents— *We have Dahntahn 4, 6 an' 9- So-oh 1-Oaklynn 4 an' 8-Shady 3- Bloomfild 2-Lahrinseville 1- Morninside 2-'Sliberty 5-Linkin 2-Squirrill 4-Swissilvale-Braddick-Souside3-Allentahn 2-MaunWorshintin 1-Ma-lebinin 5-Kerrick 2-Baldwin-Cassel Shannin'- Micke-eez Rox-Sheerdin'-Norside 2, 5 an' 6-Troy-ill-an' Etner open...Who's where?*

When done according to protocol, it was a fair system. In the real world, it did not always work that way. Many dispatchers were ex-cab drivers, and they had their buddies. Airport trips, railroad crews, and other lucrative rides were often rumored to be exchanged for donations to a dispatcher's favorite charity—often the dispatcher's personal benevolence foundation, or even something as simple as a couple of cold ones after work at Kelly's, up the street from the garage. Most drivers did not play the game, but it was what it was.

Besides the radio, there were other sources for finding fares. Although we were not exactly New York, random street hailing remained a possibility. Taxi stands near major hotels were popular spots to occupy, reliable sources for steady streams of trips. For most drivers, the goal was a trip to The Promised Land—Greater Pittsburgh Airport. The airport, Amtrak Station, and Greyhound and Trailways bus terminals were strategic spots for profitable pick-ups. The Promised Land, seventeen miles northwest of the city, was the busiest, where any trip back to the city was never a bad trip, or if lucky—remember, luck is only a small factor on this job—high paying rides to distant counties, even over state lines, were always possible.

Another excellent revenue source, far more prevalent in previous decades than today, were companies, like Bell Telephone, providing their workers with taxi vouchers for safe transport home after late shifts. At Amtrak, there was a red, direct line telephone—imagine the *Bat-Phone*—enabling travel-weary train passengers to pick up and instantly order a cab. In the late evening hours, cabbies gathered at that phone, awaiting their bat signal. When the phone rang, about ten minutes before the workers' shifts ended, each driver in the queue was assigned to a randomly selected trip number corresponding to each employee for that evening. These were popular trips. Each was a sure thing, paid with a company voucher ensuring a 15% tip, and some employees added extra cash, usually a buck or two. We knew nobody was going to rob us, kill us, run on us, act obnoxious, or be in a drunken stupor.

Fast forward to today—how many employers would even dream of offering such a benefit to their workforce? We can always long for our *Checkered Past.*

Electronic Meter and Flag Meter models used in Yellow Cabs

CHAPTER 4

Yellow Cab U

August 1977

Summer rolled by quickly, as summers always do. The taxi business was one with a relentless, unforgiving learning curve. This was no easy job to master; there was no blueprint for success. While my outward goal to earn money for a college education was successful, this occupation provided the unexpected, priceless fringe benefit of an education unattainable from any course, lecture, or textbook.

I was enthralled with the randomness and unpredictability of taxi life. While anxious and excited about attending Penn State that fall, part of me would oddly miss my side job. I was delighted to learn that by simply applying for a "withdrawal card" from the union, I could drive during term breaks, as well next summer. For me, this was a no-brainer, so I did just that.

As the summer wound down, I reluctantly closed the Greengrocer chapter of my work life. Working in a small store taught me a great deal about business practices, especially the importance of customer service. Leaving was quite difficult to do, as I had become a part of the store, and it a part of me. I realized this was a necessary break up, as I would soon be living 140 miles away.

Working evenings and late nights provided a shifting balance of risk and reward. The streets of Pittsburgh after dark offered ample opportunity for misadventure and excitement, sometimes embraced, often un-welcomed. Night shifts meant missing good times with friends, but I loved having the independence to choose when *not* to work. In the evening, there was less traffic, less restriction to movement than on dayshift, while tips became more generous as the nights wore on. There was a higher volume of trips to the airport during the daylight hours, but evenings offered a steady flow of arriving flights. Many cabbies, perhaps the majority, make their living primarily by *shifting*—deadheading empty to the airport. When the airport is moving, it becomes a reliable and safe source for easy money.

An early advantage was having my dad, who had driven for several years, as a source of cab driving advice. He tipped me off on where to *play*—the busiest areas to work, when to expect steady radio trips, and strategic times to shift to the airport. Although he and I both were nonsmokers—I went through a brief phase of cigarette-gagging in my early teens—Dad educated me on the importance of being in possession of a lighter and packs of matches when driving a taxi. Back when smoking was not the morally bankrupt, politically incorrect activity it is today, I learned to readily assist in lighting my passenger's smoking instrument. For men, I handed them the matches, and said, "go ahead, keep them." For women, I would light their smokes with a lighter if I could safely do so. And, yes, I enjoyed the momentary intimacy of lighting a cigarette for an attractive woman.

Fortunately, etiquette has evolved when it comes to smoking. I never relished breathing in second-hand smoke and have always prided myself on keeping a clean cab. Smoking is now, at least theoretically, prohibited. People, in general, do not want to enter a taxi, or any other place of business, and leave with their clothing smelling like an ashtray. Most smokers today are courteous enough to respect that lighting up is unwelcome within the confines of a taxicab. Occasionally, though, people will argue, rationalize— "I'll hold it out the window," or negotiate— "I'll give you a big tip." My answer is a consistent "NO!" In post-Checker cab-culture, a clean, comfortable, smoke-free ride can be a tremendous asset, for the driver's health, as well as his income.

The summer of '77 was truly an eye-opener. While thoroughly convinced I was this mature, seasoned, all- knowing, young adult, taxi driving constantly brought me back to earth as the naïve, untested teenager I was. I somehow thought of myself as worldly, even though I had rarely ever left Pittsburgh, let alone my comfortable little corners of the world within it. Yes, I studied psychology and criminology at Penn State, but was also in the process of undergoing intense, thorough field training at *"The University of Yellow Cab, Pittsburgh Campus."*

While retaining much knowledge from the *Introduction to Saint Clair Village- 101* class, I still occasionally got burnt on fares, but learned not to repeat risking my life trying to recover them. Sometimes, it would be a drunk who had not enough or no money at all. And there were the runners. People jumping out without paying were not limited to housing projects. I recall three guys in their twenties I picked up at the William Penn, an upscale hotel, and drove to Whitehall, a well-to-do suburb. As I stopped the taxi, both doors flew open, and they were off to the races. I later found out that this same group had successfully burnt other drivers. The worst part was that I picked up the same three scofflaws about a year later. Only after history repeated itself, did I remember them. Curses; foiled again!

Yes, there were the negative aspects of this job, but the positives outweighed them. I was fascinated by the variety of people who took turns occupying my back seat on any given night. Pittsburgh was a city of neighborhoods, each with its own unique qualities, but the human element was most interesting. One on one, I found most people to be decent, even nice! Even more intriguing were the interactions between groups within the cab. While my focus remained on the road, I could not resist the sporadic eavesdrop. Even a large, boxy taxicab can become a tiny space. The exchanges between couples were anything but boring, particularly when testing the waters in the early stages of a relationship. There were groups of men on their way to strip clubs, bragging about what they were going to do when they got there. Businesspeople riding to dinner at upscale restaurants tearing through their expense accounts. I recall Sunday night trips from the airport, ears wide open as attorneys and consultants strategized their game plans for the big Monday morning meeting. This was a whole new world opening to me, nothing short of fascinating, and often, entertaining.

And there was the other side of life. In the seventies and eighties, the Liberty Avenue section of Downtown was famous for strip-bars, gay bars, massage parlors, sex shops, and street walkers. At first, I found myself transfixed by this slice of Pittsburgh and its cast of characters. I could not wait to tell my friends about driving the hooker to her next cheap trick. There was a gay couple, dressed in *total S and M mode;* leather vests, riding boots, top hats—one even carried a small whip! Or Starr, emphatic about her two *r's,* an enticing, buxom blonde who labored at one of those respectable, all night massage therapy studios, with her sweet lemony-strawberry scent who flirtingly called me baby. Starr always happily ended my nights with a generous twenty- dollar bill for her seven- dollar ride. While this was all fun and intriguing, it could get old quickly...except for Starr!

One hot August night, I felt overwhelmed by the weirdo crowd. After a string of fares involving drunks, drag queens, loud mouths, bad tippers, or combinations of more than one of the above, I was particularly irritated. I cruised past the William Penn taxi stand, where three cabs sat idle with little visible activity around them. As I drove through a quiet downtown, a middle- aged gentleman with salt and pepper hair, glasses, and thick moustache calmly flagged me down.

"Thank God," I muttered, "someone *normal* looking."

I slowed the taxi to a halt. My newest client quickly opened the front door and sat shotgun. Most drivers perceive this as an invasion of our workspace. Unless the back seat is completely occupied, or the person has a physical impairment which makes it difficult to sit in the back, we cabbies prefer our passengers to enjoy the spacious comforts of the rear seat.

"How are you doing? Where we headed to, sir?"

"Do you know Allentown, up Arlington Avenue?"

Still relatively new, I had a vague idea, but was unsure. "You can show me the way you'd like me to go."

Allentown is a small neighborhood on the southern slopes of Pittsburgh, not to be confused with Allentown, PA, a rust belt city in the state's northeast. We crossed the Smith-field Street Bridge and wound our way up Arlington Avenue, a long curving hill with live trolley tracks, offering striking, scenic vistas of the city. Along the way, my passenger volunteered that he was from California and doing a fellowship at Duquesne University. This sounded impressive to my young and naïve self. As the conversation evolved, he turned to me and asked, "So, are you *big*?"

Not accurately reading the room, I assumed *big* to be some cool, West Coast buzzword. Not wanting to appear ignorant, I replied, "Sure, I guess so."

Within seconds, my normal, average passenger reached across the seat, his left hand aiming towards my lap. My right hand divorced the steering wheel, evolving into a fist, firmly contacting his face and forcing his eyewear upward. "What the fuck is wrong with you?"

"Well, I thought…"

"Get the fuck out of here— and pay me!"

I don't remember if I got a tip—nor did I care. I decided to call it an early night soon after *that* educational experience.

Arlington Avenue

CHAPTER 5

Crafton Park

August 1977

U nfazed by the previous creepy encounter, I returned to work the following evening. I began to realize that Pittsburgh, a good-sized city, was in many ways, just a big, small town. I learned that like the three stooges who ran on me in Whitehall, this "gentleman" was an occasional rider who had previously practiced the same mode of operation with other younger drivers. He always purported himself as a visitor to the city, here for a conference, convention, internship, meeting, or seminar, and rode to the Allentown area. As I became more demographically enlightened with our city's myriad of neighborhoods, I determined that a side street in Allentown, an area on a downward slide, would be an unlikely destination for a tourist.

Driving a cab in this big-small town, it was just my luck to again encounter creepy- seminar-up-the-hill to Allentown guy several months later. At first, I failed to recognize him, having made many incident-free trips to Allentown, and hauling numerous other creepy people since. However, as soon as he began his routine, it was a total recall. This time, I stopped him in his tracks, informing him I will gladly deliver him to the destination of his choice if he keeps his hands to himself. The trip ended without incident—even topped off with a decent tip!

Another lesson learned in those early days at *Yellow Cab University* was how frequently people altered their behavior within the confines of a taxi, particularly after a few drinks. Even without the aid of any mind- altering substances, many tended to be less self-conscious or guarded than they otherwise would be. Some, especially if they resided in a different city, viewed the cab driver as someone who they would unlikely encounter again, feeling entitled to behave in any way they wished.

Others saw taxi drivers as so far beneath them on the societal totem pole, that it didn't matter what they said or how they acted. Most often, it was simply a case of folks out for a night on the town and it was time to let loose. The taxi ride was a small part of that experience. As long as they did not get overly obnoxious, or emit unwelcome bodily fluids, I was happy to play a minor role player in their evening adventures.

As my first summer of driving neared its conclusion, I answered a radio call shortly after midnight at a Liberty Avenue strip bar. For bar calls, the dispatcher would often attach a name, identifying the passenger. At other times, he would simply say "for the bar" or "for the door," signifying the bartender or doorman had placed the order. This trip was from *Stage 966* "for the bar." I hoped that it was for one of the dancers, but it seemed too early for their evening to conclude; probably some dirty old men out getting their jollies.

Pulling up to the "966", the only thing exceeding my surprise was my delight as I counted four alluring "older" women. In my diluted, naïve, twenty-year -old mind, mid-thirties to early forties meant *old*. Three of the ladies piled into the back seat, while one, an attractive, petite, brunette with a body that most younger women could only wish for, asked if I would "mind" her company up front. While I usually prefer my clientele to enjoy the luxury of the spacious back seat, this time, of course, I didn't mind a bit!

"Whew...we got us a youngie!" proclaimed one of the ladies from the back.

Slightly baffled, somewhat intimidated *(a youngie?)*, I made a lame attempt at a humorous response. "Hey, I'm older and wiser than I may appear..."

The group, it turned out, was enjoying a girls' night out, celebrating the newly granted freedom from the bonds of marriage for one of the ladies—a divorce party! They went for a nice dinner out, did a little barhopping, and decided to cap off their evening at a strip bar, a bold endeavor for women at the time. We were heading for Crafton, a bedroom community bordering Pittsburgh's West End. I found myself enjoying the sights, scents, and sounds of my four passengers, happy I was outnumbered. They were all slightly drunk, flirting, and laughing the entire trip.

Of the ladies in the back, one was happily married, one happily single, and, the guest of honor, freshly divorced. Becky, my front seat companion, was also married, but confided to not being especially thrilled about it lately. I must admit I enjoyed the attention. I spent the entire summer working two jobs, emotionally reeling from a previous break up with a long- time girlfriend and had not dated anyone since. It had been a while.

As we approached the Crafton area, one of the ladies suggested, and the others concurred, continuing their evening adventure at Crafton Park and "having some fun with the cab driver."

Golly, I didn't even know Crafton had a park! Assuming they were only kidding around, I played along. I dropped off the first two, who lived only a few doors down from one another. They pooled some money for the fare, tipping me quite generously. Now, it was just the fresh divorcee and the pretty, little—married—woman, whose position on the front seat was notably closer to me than when the ride began. I tried maintaining my *semi*-professionalism.

"Okay girls, who's next, where do we live?"

They joked about the park again, while I wondered if this joke was only a joke. Becky directed me through a couple more turns on back streets, eventually pulling in front of a small apartment house.

"This is me!" The evening's honoree leaned over and hugged her friend in the front seat, then turned to me with a surprise kiss on the cheek and a playful wink. "Bye Howie; take good care of our little Becky!"

I continued basking with delight; first time I had ever received a good-night kiss from a passenger! I tried appearing calm and cool, with limited success.

Becky inched closer, lightly rubbing my arm. Although I could hear faint whispers of caution from the rational side of my brain, I was still a horny, hormone-raging college kid. Yeah, she's maybe fifteen, twenty years older than me, married— kids; never even asked; a little buzzed, but we were only goofing around, nothing was going to happen.

We made a couple more turns, again traveling down a main road.

"Turn left here, honey..."

I followed her instructions, steering into a small, wooded area, past a plain wooden sign: CRAFTON PARK. *Uh-oh!* Next thing I knew, we parked in a dark, secluded lot, my lips locked with those of an alluring, hot-blooded woman. "I'll really miss this job!" I thought as we made out for several pleasurable minutes. Our encounter progressed with an awkward tumble into the back seat, both my shirt and Becky's halter-type top becoming seat drapery.

I now can only wish this movie had ended with an *"X,"* or at least an *"R"* rating; alas, it barely qualified for a *"PG."* Something inside made me call a time out on what could have been a night of fantasy fulfillment—*random, passionate sex with a beautiful older woman!* I told Becky that I didn't want to be a part of something she may eventually regret. She wanted to continue our encounter, but I—as in *Idiot*—talked her out of it. I thought I was being noble, recalling how it felt to be cheated on, not wanting to inflict that on someone else. Or was I ever-so slightly intimidated; was she out of my league?

We regrouped and awkwardly laughed the whole thing off. Re-entering the front seat, using the doors this time, we drove away from the park. Three minutes later, we stopped on a quiet suburban street in the shadows of a fine red brick home. I received a quick peck on the cheek, a warm smile, and a quietly mouthed "thank you." And she was gone.

I headed back towards Pittsburgh, that big-small-town. While I have had innumerable re-encounters with countless passengers over the years, Pittsburgh can easily transform into a lonely place. I never saw Becky again. Occasionally, when driving past the sign reading "Crafton Park," I smile and fondly remember that hot, late August night.

And, yes, her name was changed to protect the innocent.

CHAPTER 6

Withdrawal

1977-1979

Summer reached its inevitable conclusion, completing my initiation into the taxi world. Despite the bumps and bruises along the way, my rookie season at Yellow Cab turned out to be a financial success. While not getting rich, I was pleased to earn enough to fund my fall tuition, room, board, and even books!

"What? You haven't packed all your shit yet! Are you fucking kidding me?" screamed my buddy, Marty, his eyes widening with only *partial* amazement.

The time had come to leave for Penn State! Marty, beginning his senior year, agreed to ride along and help acclimatize me to my new environment. The plan was to head up in *Big Red*, my 1969 Oldsmobile Delta 88 convertible, topless— *The car, not us!* Always the procrastinator, I had barely organized or packed any of my belongings. Both excited and uneasy about this brand- new phase of life, I had no clue what to expect. Having logged two successful years at the local campus, up to this point, I'd never visited the main campus. I can't recall any other students I've known not even visiting their campus at least once prior to enrolling.

First, we loaded Marty's stuff, along with the flimsy suitcase and a few boxes I had packed that morning. I tossed the remainder of my clothing and odds- and- ends with marginal accuracy from my third- floor bedroom window into and around the awaiting top-down convertible. Poor Marty, positioned on the sidewalk below, relayed stuff into the back-seat, while my family and neighbors looked on with, again, only *partial* amazement. This was undoubtably the moment in life when I eliminated the moving and storage industry as a career option.

I had mixed emotions about leaving home. It was time to bid farewell to my family and be on the way. The varying degrees of emotional goodbyes from family members were each warmer and fuzzier than I reciprocated at the time. Having spent little time at home during the previous couple of years, I would strangely miss the option of being able to return there at will.

Although it was a picture-perfect late summer morning, we wound up driving with the convertible top up, thanks to the disorganized array of stuff scattered about the back seat. Marty insisted on indoctrinating me to some obscure singer, *Bruce Springsteen,* on Big Red's built in eight track tape-deck. "Pretty good stuff," I thought. Traveling through the scenic mountains of Central Pennsylvania, I felt optimistic about the immediate future. After three hours of slicing and dicing such fine towns as Nanty Glo, Lilly, Tyrone, and Port Mathilda, the campus appeared on the horizon.

Marty directed me to the dormitory. I was surprised that most other arriving students were chauffeured by their parents. Marty schooled me that keeping a car on campus was useless until you needed to travel a significant distance from the university. Once staking claim to a coveted space in the vast student parking area, it was time to bid adieu to my motorized companion.

Nittany, my assigned housing section, consisted of a series of long, single-storied, beige, and green stucco buildings with few amenities. Decades earlier, they served our country with distinction as army barracks. They resembled housing projects, considered to be the bottom of the barrel of on campus living quarters. The one good thing was that the majority of the rooms were singles, meaning no roommates. At first, I was disappointed with my newest living arrangement. I hoped to be paired with a roommate, as I was not an outgoing person and knew hardly anyone on campus. A roommate would at least *force* me to get to know someone new. Marty, who had an apartment in town, said I was lucky to get a single. He pointed out how you did not have to be thrown into a small room with someone who farted, snored, or had little in common with you. And, if you were lucky enough to have "company," there was no need to plot out details and strategies with a roommate.

Most of the students in our building, Nittany#40, were friendly and welcoming. There were guys from all over the state, out of state, even Vietnam! I enjoyed the diversity of our little group. It, however, became a tad over diverse for me, when on the second day I walked down the hallway on the other half of the building. Upon introducing myself to three guys in a room, I could not help but notice the large Nazi-swastika flag adorning the wall. I made the introduction *very* brief. Most of the people in the building avoided those guys, but we all amicably co-existed.

Another good thing about living in Nittany was the free reign students had to paint and decorate their living quarters as they wished. My room was some god- awful shade of yellow. Bill, my neighbor, volunteered to assist with my interior decorating challenge. That evening, with the help of a pizza and a few beers, my room transformed to a fresh, respectable blue.

It was a huge culture shock adapting to life on an enormous university campus as a junior. Commuting to a small branch, I completed the required coursework, but remained otherwise detached from university life. Living here, I became as indigenous to the Penn State landscape as yellow cabs were to their respective city streets. Within a couple of days, classes started, and I blended in with the student populace.

Always a workaholic, I was determined to find work in State College. Thrilled to discover a specialty fruit and vegetable shop at the far end of town, I promptly filled out an application. I was surprised to find a small taxi company and applied there also. Surely, one of those places would find value in my wisdom and expertise and hire me! Well… they surely did not. The legendary Penn State Diner offered a job as a short order cook, even though I told them that I had no clue how to cook. In fact, I had no idea how to crack an egg! I accepted the offer but wimped out before my first scheduled shift. Fortunately, my buddy, Bill, who had worked the previous summer as a line cook, bailed me out and reported for my shift. He wound up working there for six months thereafter. Me? I ended up at Arby's, a thirty- minute trek from my dorm. Between work and classes, I stayed busy. While not a difficult job, wearing the brown polyester uniform with orange and yellow flowered trim, walking home at two-in-the-morning reeking of fry grease with an eight o'clock class looming, and the monotony of slicing cheap roast beef for drunken college kids made me miss my summer job.

The fall term flew by. Penn State had ten -week trimesters rather than traditional fifteen- week semesters. I looked forward to driving Yellow Cab during Thanksgiving break. Prior to leaving for school, I obtained a Union Withdrawal Card, which allowed me to return to work anytime, maintaining my good standing with the company. I wound up driving every night of the break, but for one to hang out with friends, one with family. Yes, making money was the prime attraction, especially good for a student, yet something else kept drawing me back to this world. My Pittsburgh and Penn State friends were always intrigued by my taxi misadventures, and I never minded satisfying their curiosity.

I returned in December 1977 for winter term, once again, working Yellow Cab through Christmas break— even New Year's Eve! In the spring, I accepted a counseling internship at a Pittsburgh facility for troubled teens. The unpaid practicum offered a new excuse to re-enlist as a "weekend warrior" for the cab company.

Perhaps that little card which kept allowing me to return to my summer job was called a *Withdrawal Card* for a reason. Like an addict, I could never get enough, craving just one more dose, another fix of taxi life. What troubled me was while finally doing real work in my chosen field, I felt more motivated to work my side job. This was not part of any plan.

I spent the summer of 1978 driving full time. Upon returning for senior year, I landed a work-study job two nights a week, staffing the front desk of a girl's dormitory on the overnight shift. I also volunteered on a peer-counseling hotline, listening to college students whine on and on about how difficult their college lives were. While my own life was far from perfect, I wanted to be empathetic. However, I could not help noticing how often my once soft bleeding-heart toughened up and stopped bleeding. Perhaps the cab was altering my personality. Who knew?

Nonetheless, I earned my degree, a Bachelor of Science in Individual and Family Studies, finishing with a decent 3.37 Grade Point Average. For my final term, I took the minimal nine credits I needed to graduate, worked nowhere on or off campus, did no volunteer work, just hung out, drinking beer, playing Frisbee, opening a book on rare occasions. It was the easiest I ever had in life, earning an unimpressive 2.0 (one B, one C and one D) GPA. Had I upped just *one* of those grades, I would have graduated on the Dean's List. I was burnt-out, it sucked being me. I remember sitting in the dining hall with a group of friends on the final day of classes. As we reflected and said our farewells, I looked up, declaring, "I think I want to change my major!"

The line was met with laughter from all. Truth be told, I studied my ass off for the past four years, accumulating more than my money's worth of an education which I will forever value and cherish, but there was no plan. My mind filled with apprehension and uncertainty. Should I try graduate school, maybe a master's in criminal justice? Psychology? One professor suggested taking the Law Boards. I always had a head for business, yet never sniffed a business course, not even as an elective. The idea of over-the-road truck driving was enticing, a chance to see the country. I had a knack for writing, but never took any classes in journalism or creative writing. Would have loved to teach history or sociology but lacked certification. Here I was, 21, armed with a degree, wondering what to do *if* I grew up.

I did not want to return to school for the time being. I was fortunate enough to have no student debt, as I was able to earn sufficient money to pay for my education as I went along. *Thank you, Yellow Cab!* During my senior year, I assisted with a program within Penn State's College of Human Development, helping students prepare cover-letters and resumes for their internships. Ironically, here I was, ready to join the real world, with no fresh resume of my own, no semblance of a battle plan. Was it supposed to end up this way?

So, once again, with no better place to be, I appeared at the cage of Yellow's East Liberty Garage, flashing my well-worn Withdrawal Card, while my hard-earned B.S. Degree languished at home embarking on an extensive dust collection. "Driver 505, ready to work!"

Freddy, the ever-present cage dispatcher, just smiled, shaking his head. "They always come back—they just keep coming back."

Author's Note: *Fred Lewis, the retired Yellow Cab cashier, passed on November 15, 2013, the day of the completion of first draft of this chapter.*

Penn State Nittany Dorms

CHAPTER 7

A Fish Story

Spring, 1979

It was nine o'clock on a Saturday evening when dispatched to *Poli's* as the second taxi of a two- cab order for a large group. My mind flashed back to the last call I answered from this popular seafood restaurant and got beat out of an expensive fare on my inaugural cab- driving rodeo. I laughed it off, now old and wise enough to realize the bulk of these trips from high end dining spots involved businesspeople chewing away at generous expense accounts.

As I pulled up, the first taxi was loaded and on the move with the outlines of four heads visible in the back window and the extended arm of the shotgun rider holding an oversized lit cigar out the front window. A party of four, three men flanked by a stunning, head-turning brunette with long wavy hair and well-fitted designer jeans, approached.

A man in his thirties with neatly manicured mid-length deep brown hair claiming the front seat seemed familiar,

53

someone I had seen somewhere, but unable to place. A towering, sharply dressed, African American man and a stocky middle- aged man with thinning, grayish hair, and wire-framed glasses sandwiched the attractive woman in the back seat. The older man appeared recognizable, but again, I could not recall if we had ever crossed paths. The tall guy did not ring a bell but could have easily passed for a basketball player.

"Hyatt Pittsburgh, please," directed the shotgun passenger.

"Yes, Sir," I nodded, hitting the Parkway for the quick jaunt to town. One aspect of this job I was beginning to appreciate was the continuing variety of attractive women taking turns occupying my back seat. Sure, most were out of my league, but I learned to savor eye candy without staring or creeping. The lady in the rearview mirror seemed recognizable, I knew her from somewhere—maybe? These folks had obviously enjoyed some beverages and were laughing and joking around. As the woman spoke, her big brown eyes lit up the cab. *Wow, holy shit, is that who I think it is?*

The box office smash hit *Grease* had recently concluded its successful run in Pittsburgh and across the country. I peeked in the mirror once more to be sure before disrupting the group's banter. "Oh, my G-d, it's...it's you...you're Rizzo... from that movie!" I felt like an instant idiot.

She looked up; she had a sweet smile. "Yes, that was definitely me."

I told her how much I loved that movie (I did like the film— love was a stretch), adding that she was my favorite character. I did not know how to tell her I had no idea what her real name was.

She was congenial, informing me they were in town filming another potential blockbuster, something to do with fish and basketball. It was about a backward city (who—us?) and its misfit basketball team. Hey, I thought that guy was a basketball player!

"I'll be first in line to see that movie!" I promised my cab-load as we pulled into the Hyatt's driveway. The man in front kept giving me a *are you kidding* look as if I should have readily identified him, but I could not. I wish I had asked everyone who they were. But as they were about to exit, I got up the nerve to ask Rizzo one more question. "This is awkward but, what's your real name?"

She smiled, holding out her hand. "I'm Stockard Channing; what's yours?"

"Uh, well, uh, Howie," I blurted, struggling to extract my foot from my mouth. She gave me more of a palm squeeze than a handshake; I liked that.

As they exited, the guy in front (where have I seen him before?) handed me a fin for the $4.10 meter. "Keep the rest, buddy."

The Fish That Saved Pittsburgh, when released, received heavy local press coverage. One article revealed that Chevy Chase of Saturday Night Live fame was initially cast but backed out. Was that he who gave me the 90- cent tip? *Hey Chevy, if you ever read this, can you let me know?* I never solved the mystery of the two other guys, but they may well have been Jonathan Winters and Meadowlark Lemon, who both were in the movie. I will never know for sure, another uncracked case.

I was never first in line to see the movie. In fact, as I recollect this so many years later, I have yet to see it. Call me a procrastinator. The reviews were not kind; *The Fish* was more of a bust than a blockbuster, but Ms. Channing, it was my pleasure to meet you. I hope you enjoyed your stay in our big- small town.

CHAPTER 8

Tipology: An Inexact Science

"Please-select-your-tip-amount," directs that familiar, yet anonymous robotic female voice from the taxicab's backseat mounted self-serve credit card reader.

Marwan, an engineering student from Qatar experiencing his first American taxi ride, stares at the screen with a bewildered look. "What is *tip*?" he wonders. This is uncustomary in his culture. He looks up, observing the cab driver's expression in the rear- view mirror, an eyeroll of impatience. Unsure of his next move, Marwan reluctantly presses the 15% option, rewarding the taxi-man with a $7.50 bonus, observing as his airport fare rolls from $50.00 to $57.50.

***

Tipping is as ingrained within our culture as apple pie. One who has never encountered a slice of this crusty, gooey-sugary treat would not be sure whether to use a fork, spoon, fingers, or even eat it at all. Uncertainty often occurs at the tipping moment of truth to those unfamiliar with American gratuity etiquette. And, yes, to people who are intrinsically cheap.

The idea of tipping is near and dear to my heart. I vividly recall the first money I ever earned came in the form of a tip. When I was six, our family lived in East Liberty, an area not known for its wealth. On nearby North Highland Avenue was a small supermarket, "Giant Eagle." Today, Giant Eagle, fondly known to us Pittsburghers as *Jynt Iggels*, is the dominant force in Pittsburgh's retail food scene.

Back to my childhood memories. I noticed when shoppers exited Giant Eagle's automatic doors, which I deemed to be wonders of technology, some of the older neighborhood kids took turns wheeling customers' shopping carts to the parking lot and helping load their groceries into the cars. The adults rewarded the industrious children with a tip, usually a coin or two. I thought this was great and decided to join one Saturday morning. At first, I felt intimidated, being the smallest, youngest, and only white kid in the group. Thankfully, Mike, the tallest and de-facto leader of the operation, allocated me a small market share. Most folks tipped a dime, some fifteen cents, occasionally even a quarter! And thus, began my initiation into the tipping world.

In 1967 (yes, I'm *that* old), we moved to the Squirrel Hill neighborhood. To earn money, my older brother, Ben, and I went door-to-door, shouldering three essential tools—a shovel, an ice- crusher and a well-worn broom. Heavy snow events always spelled money for us. If we did a good job clearing people's sidewalks and driveways, there it was again-- the tip! It was at this point in life when I developed a great love for *Campbell's Tomato Soup*. Flinging snow and ice around for six or seven hours in freezing temperatures can have that effect.

Shortly thereafter, I began a long run of newspaper delivery, another entry into that mystical world of tipping. Many of my paper route customers would tip when I had to play the role of weekly collection agent. These were the *keep the change* tips, individually never great sums of money, but collectively more than chump change. The Christmas holiday season was an exciting time for paper carriers. Most people threw an extra five, or, ten- dollar bill, one lady even tipped crisp, new twenties each year—huge money for a twelve- year- old!

Most of my subscribers tucked my little bonus inside a card, often a simple Merry Christmas or Happy Chanukah envelope. While enthralled with the monetary rewards, it meant so much more when they added a note, appreciating good service and wishing me well. I fondly recall one elderly gentleman in a modest house, who never tipped during the year, waiting on his porch at 5AM on a frigid morning, personally handing me a card containing a crisp, clean one-dollar bill. I surprised myself when I felt the same level of gratitude towards this man as the $10 and $20 tippers.

In addition to the home delivery of newspapers, I sometimes hustled them on the streets. These were the high roller tips — at least percentage wise. The Holiday Editions, with their fifteen-cent cover price, were frequently paid with a quarter and simultaneous "keep the change." Does not sound rich, but 67%--not a bad tip!

I liked the newspaper gig so much that I took on more routes, delivering well into my high school years. While most of my paper route career was with the early morning *Post Gazette*, for a year, I delivered an afternoon route of the now defunct *Pittsburgh Press* along Murray Avenue in Greenfield, including its small business district. I always ordered extra papers to peddle inside the three local bars along the route. My favorite customer, Old Man Homer, a local businessman, often doubled as my pro-bono financial adviser as he rewarded me with a generous 50 cents while enjoying his daily beverages at *The Coop*. "Save your money, buy a Cadillac!" or, "Buy yourself a house and lot!" While I had never owned a Caddy, I heeded Mr. Homer's advice, purchasing a house *and lot* years later.

It's been over fifty years since I hijacked my last shopping cart, over forty since long- tossing my last newspaper. I wish subsequent generations had the same opportunities as I did. My newspaper is now delivered by a man in a car, who incidentally, has been my "paperboy" for twenty-plus years. I have only met him in passing a few times, probably wouldn't even recognize him if standing behind him in the check-out lines at *Jynt Iggles*. But I never forget to mail him that card with a bonus check each December.

***

The conclusion of this tip scientific study? Tip. Tip well. Your server. Your bartender. They earn it. Don't forget your barber, hairdresser, doorman, pizza guy, newspaper carrier—if he is not yet obsolete—the shuttle driver, limo driver...and, of course, your taxi driver!

CHAPTER 9

Bittner

January 1980

I f we ever classified taxis as institutions of higher learning, he certainly would have earned the title of distinguished professor. His formal name was William Coleman Bittner, but his passengers and peers referred to him as *Bulgy*, or, simply, *Bittner*. I remember my dad introducing him one evening at the Amtrak taxi rotunda as Mr. Bittner, and am sure Dad mentioned my name was Howie. From that point forward, for him, I was forever "young man." While in direct conversation, I always addressed him as "Mr. Bittner." In my mind, he remains eternally enshrined as Bittner.

On this biting cold and brutally quiet Tuesday night, there were few taxis patrolling the city, but even fewer people out on the streets. Still a relative newcomer to this lifestyle, my theory of the conjunction of single digit temperatures and bone chilling winds translating into an endless multitude of cab trips turned out to be dead wrong. Cruising slowly along

Liberty Avenue, all I observed were a few courageous souls huddling at bus stops and a single, determined, if not desperate hooker seeking temporary employment. My big warm yellow taxi interested no one. The cab radio was almost silent as well. At least the Checker's heat worked well. A good heater was not always a guarantee.

While working heat was never a constant, the late evening Bell Telephone employee trips were. From 11:00 PM onward, various departments of the phone company offered their loyal workers complimentary cab rides home. Because of the high volume of these trips, they were dispatched first to taxis waiting in a queue at the Amtrak one block from the phone company through a direct phone line, freeing up the two-way radio for other calls.

At 10:42 PM, I rolled up the meticulously maintained brown- bricked circular driveway of Amtrak's Pennsylvania Station, our majestic train depot. There was only a single cab parked ahead of me; #281--Good old Bittner.

Bittner was always prepared with a fresh story to tell. Most were quite entertaining, even if not always believable. He was the cab- driver's cabby, unfailingly geared up for a lively debate, available for unsolicited free advice, or an eye-opening history lesson—Bulgy Bittner was one of a kind.

Leaning against the front fender of his cab, Bittner seemed oblivious to the bitter weather. Not wishing to be rude, I had a thorough appreciation for the hot air circulating from my cab's heating vents. For the moment, I preferred that hot air to Bittner's, but could already sense his acknowledgement as he tipped the brim of his cap in my direction. Eye contact. I had no choice but to join him.

"Cold one, eh, Mr. Bittner?" It was the best I could come up with for the moment.

"How ya doin' there, young man?" Before I could respond, it was evident he needed to share some pertinent information. "*Veal-Parma-zahn!*" Bittner proclaimed, adjusting his thick, black framed glasses northward. "Have you ever tried veal parmazahn?"

Never one to be confused with a gourmet guru, I might have ordered it once at Del's Bar, a couple of miles up the road in nearby Bloomfield. I cautiously nodded.

"Well, then, lemme tell ya," he pointed downward toward the bus station across Liberty Avenue. "Right in there, the Greyhound cafeteria, ya gotta try it—the finest veal-parma-zahn I ever tasted!"

"Uh, wow, that good, huh?" I shivered, going with the program. It was impossible to dislike Bulgy Bittner. He towered over me, an easy six- foot- two or three, sporting a well-earned beer belly, a rite of passage from seven decades of a life well lived. Although Yellow Cab specified no official uniform code, Bittner always wore pristine pressed navy or black work pants, a light blue shirt, a dark blue jacket emblazoned with a red and white Yellow Cab Company circular logo, topped off by his trademark blue, Yellow Cab pilot's hat. He was a constant reminder that this was truly a profession, not a casual gig.

"Ya- know, young man, like I told ya, I've been around a long time, heh! Lived in New York, out west for a while, done a lotta travlin'. But tonight—that veal… ain't had nothin' that good in a helluva long time! Who'd a thunk it, right there in the Greyhound?"

"Well, I guess I'll have to..." The red phone rang loudly, saved by the bell! Bittner promptly picked up, repeated his order number, and passed the baton to me.

"1-3-7," I recited my cab number to the dispatcher, who reciprocated with a corresponding trip number. "TSPS#2," I echoed, handing off the receiver to another driver who had just arrived.

For the Bell Telephone trips, the drivers parked the cabs in front of the building along Grant Street and congregated in the lobby awaiting the workers, mostly female telephone information operators, to finish their shifts. By now, nine or ten cabs were on the scene, several drivers encircling Bittner as he provided his vivid and detailed *Veal Parm* dissertation. Classic Bittner.

The first wave of workers poured from the opening elevator doors. "A-T&T-6... TSPS-5, E-2-..." The Bell people sought out their matching cabbies. As Bittner found his trip, as usual other familiar folks exchanged greetings. *Hey, Bulgy!... Happy New Years, Mr. Bittner!...* I found my trip, TSPS-2, an elderly woman from Munhall named Theresa.

After dutifully opening my back door for Theresa, something many drivers fail to do, but Bittner always did, I put the cab in gear and headed down Grant Street towards the parkway.

"I bet you must know old man Bulgy," Theresa took an educated guess. It turns out she knew him prior to his cab driving days. "He was from 'out my way,' worked over at U.S. Steel Homestead Works for years, married for a long while, but things turned south. Bulgy, he was always such a character. Most of us Bell girls love riding with him, hearing his crazy stories."

"I don't know him that well, but you're right; he is a piece of work for sure. But you can't help but like the guy!" I decided against attempting to retell the Greyhound-Veal saga; she without a doubt will eventually hear about it.

Bittner began his taxi career in the early 1960s, following his divorce, walking away from the mill, and becoming a world traveler. He settled into the job and defined it. Those who knew him well told me he was an avid reader and a history buff. I remember one night at the airport, he proudly showed off a handwritten letter from a famous writer (I can't recall who) praising Bittner's insights and analytics of her book. He lived a block and a half from the garage, in the East Liberty YMCA on South Whitfield Street. Like the surrounding neighborhood, the YMCA's best days were history. A structure of undeniable distinguished architecture, it served as a rooming house for transients, often men who had lost their way trying to find their path back into life. Bittner was different, one of few people who lived there for years, by choice. He had a room full of books; it was all he needed. "Hey, it's good and clean, the rent is cheap, I don't need a car, I'm at work in five minutes, and the library is right next door. It doesn't get much better than that."

Bittner was without a doubt one of the all-time great storytellers who ever sat behind the wheel of a cab. I remember one tale, which would be my honor to recount in memory of this colorful character. Please know that I could never possess the ability to express it as charmingly and elegantly as Bulgy, but here is my best shot:

It was a summer morning on a Sunday in 1970, nuttin' goin' on nowhere. I was sittin' in my cab on Oakland 5, in front of Webster Hall Hotel, readin' the Sunday Press. It was about 6:30, all I hear is birds chirpin' when there was this faint sound, like metal or steel scrapin' on the street.

I look around, don't see nuttin' at first, then doggone it, there's this guy's head peeking out of an open manhole cover in the middle of Fifth Avenue. He crawls out the opening, then starts staggerin' towards the cab. I didn't know what to think, but he comes over to my window and asks to go to the airport! It took me a second to get over my shock, so I say,"Sure, hop on in buddy."

On the way out, I had to ask, so I did; "What the hell were ya doin' in a manhole on a Sunday morning?" Turns out, he was in tahn for a weddin' and went out drinkin' afterwards, so him and his buddies climbed in there together as a joke. He was so damn drunk he fell asleep and now had to catch a morning flight home. Ya never know on this job — eh?

So, we get to the 'port quick, it's not even seven o'clock. I'm debating; should I head up to the lot and wait in line or go back to town, you know Sunday mornin' at the port ain't no great shake. As I start drivin' away from the circle, a lady comes running out the terminal, chasing my cab, yelling like I'm the last taxi left on earth!

"Where we goin,'Miss?"

She catches her breath. "What will you charge to take me to Canton, Ohio?"

I dunno, but I tell her I guess between 90 and 100 bucks, which was a helluva lot of money back then, and she hands me six twenties and says, let's do it. Two hours later, I'm empty in the middle of I don't know where, somewhere in farm country. Ya know, a wrong turn here and another there, now I'm lost. I'm lookin' for a way out, and as I cross this narrow bridge, I spot a guy in a small rowboat fishin' in the crick. So, I get out and ask how the hell can I get back home. He starts tellin' me, then stops and says,"Hey—I gotta fly outta Pittsburgh this afternoon. If you take me home to get my suitcase, I'll show you the way back and you'll save my bother-in-law a trip. I hate ridin' with that s.o.b. anyways!"

We don't even discuss price, but soon enough, we were on our way back east. He was a nice fella, not gettin' along with the wife's family, had to go on a business trip—he didn't even get dressed up properly to fly on a plane! We get to the airport; he hands over two brand new fifty-dollar bills—fifties! I'm thinkin' –whatta day! All I gotta do is head up to the waiting lot, get a trip and quit early with good money. It looked like about 30 or 40 cabs in line, so I may have to wait an hour or two for a trip back to town, I thought, when can you believe it? Another guy walks out of the terminal, flags me down. What are the odds? Maybe once, rarely twice a year do ya luck into a trip from the circle at the airport, now I get two in a row! And; how'bout this-he's goin' right to Wellesley Avenue, right there in Highland Park, a mile from the garage. Easiest and weirdest day I ever had!"

William Coleman Bittner passed at the age of a young seventy-two, likely on his own terms. His life would not end in a nursing home, not in a hospital's intensive care unit, not surrounded by family, counting out time. On Saturday evening, March 15, 1980, Bulgy entered his cab to begin his shift and suffered an apparent heart attack. Maybe his final meal was veal- parmesan; no one will ever know. His life ended in his beloved East Liberty neighborhood. I do not know if it was ever noted how this self-educated, enlightened, gentle giant who devoured so many books, would meet his fate on the Ides of March.

The Centre cab garage in East Liberty is long gone. The spot where Bittner's body was discovered has evolved into a highly coveted parking spot in the lot of a bustling Whole Foods. East Liberty's YMCA is also history, but the building was reborn into an amazing, rejuvenated *Ace Hotel*. The original off- white stone columns and architecture were restored with kid-glove care, while pristinely preserved, engraved arched lettering proclaiming *Young Men's Christian Association* above the entrance welcomes guests into the lobby.

I have never heard of any ghosts on this property, nor have I ever been a ghost enthusiast. If you ever spend a night at this old East Liberty landmark and swear you experienced a flashing glimpse of a spectacled, gray, shadowy figure lurking around an upper-floor hallway, fear not. It was certainly old Bulgy Bittner, just checking out the place. If so, this kindred spirit will not suddenly turn the place icy-cold, like those spirits portrayed in poltergeist- type movies. You would feel warmth, note a friendly smile, and if it was your lucky day, hear a wondrous story.

CHAPTER 10

The Gun Waver

March 1980

These things happen in threes. So, I've been told. This cliché refers to any trio of similar occurrences within a finite term, often sad things, even catastrophic. Death, for instance.

Aha moments are often declared when any group of three lives expire within a given period. Three rock stars perish within three months, someone somewhere surely states to any three people who will listen, "These things-they always happen in threes."

During the wonder years of my cab career, it seemed every time I answered a call at Poli's Restaurant, an adventure ensued. There was my inaugural shift, chauffeuring a lovely couple, making multiple stops all over Pittsburgh, only to have the ride end without payment in St. Clair Village, the city's most crime-ridden public housing project. Despite stupidly leaving the cab, I was fortunate to remain in one piece.

In the chronology of my Poli's adventures, this was thing number one.

Two years later, I encountered my first group of celebrity passengers, once again, from Poli's. While this was not a bad thing, it took me a few minutes to recognize Rizzo from the box-office smash *Grease*, sandwiched between two big guys in my back seat. Not horrific, but notable enough to deem book worthy—thing number two, indeed.

And then, there was this third thing, another trip originating from, you guessed — good 'ole Poli, on a crisp, frigid wintry Sunday evening.

At finer dining establishments, people awaiting taxis typically congregate outside the front of the restaurant or wait inside the lobby. For neighborhood bar calls, we routinely park and go into the bar, conferring with the barkeeper to secure our target. On this call, after both the valet attendant and hostess pleaded the fifth, it was time to check the bar.

A dozen or so people occupied high-back stools, clustered into small groups around the sizeable L-shaped bar, but for one loner sitting at the far end. "Anybody order a cab?" I said, looking at the bartender, loud enough for all to hear. The loner gestured in my direction.

"Hey, Joe, let's get this cabby a drink... an' another double for me!" he barked.

My lucky day. This happens to cab drivers more than you could ever imagine. Do you seriously want your driver to join you for a few before he drives you home? Do some drivers ever answer, "Sure, thanks?" Under oath, I'd plead the fifth on that one!

"Um, thank you, no, can't do that," I replied.

"C'mon, cabby-just one!" insisted my inebriated client.

Suddenly, the bartender became my ally. "Hey, pal, I think you've reached your limit. This man's time is his money, time to go."

I rethought whether this was an actual alliance or was I the convenient dumping ground?

The man tossed a few bills onto the bar from a noteworthy wad of cash and stumbled from the bar to a coat rack, retrieving a long, brown overcoat. His graying, blackish hair, thick dark-framed glasses, and goatee conveyed a blending first impression of a professor and used car salesman rolled into one. He staggered as he followed me out of the restaurant. I made it a point to open the cab's rear passenger side door, determining early on there was no way I wanted this bozo riding shotgun.

As I settled into the driver's seat, he introduced himself as Dr. Charlie, emphasizing the *doctor*. He continued jabbering about something I couldn't make out, not that I cared to know. All I needed to ascertain could be asked with two simple words: "Where to?"

He stared blankly for several seconds, wearing an annoyed look. "Just turn over there," he pointed left, "and hit the parkway towards *tahn*."

"Ah-right," I sighed, frustrated. I needed to know where he wanted to go, a specific destination, not slurred driving directions from an obnoxious drunk. We hadn't even begun the ride and my only thought was *whatever gets this over with.* I tried again, "sir, you need to tell me where we're headed, where you live?"

"Just get on the damn Parkway, will ya!"

Shaking my head, I threw the flag and banged a left. While I had become somewhat of an expert on handling drunks over the past couple of years, this guy was legitimately on my last nerves, doctor, or no doctor. After a few more minutes of random mumbling, Dr Charlie finally blurted out "Upper St. Clair," brightening my outlook.

Not to be confused with St. Clair Village, as in thing number one, Upper St. Clair is an affluent suburb of stately residences at the southern edge of the county, a decent trip of around 20 miles. The man continued his ranting in the back seat, the only consistently discernible words being bitch, fuck, shit, slut, and whore.

A universal law embedded in the geographical wonders of Pittsburgh is that there are always multiple ways to get from here to there. As we approached the downtown area along the Parkway, I had to interrupt the good doctor somewhere between the words fuck and whore. "Do you want to hit 79, or take Banksville through Mt Lebanon?"

He glared, "Banksville, you fuckin' idiot!"

Realizing this guy was double barrel loaded with cash along with alcohol, I chose to ignore the insult. As we crossed the Fort Pitt Bridge, his verbiage suddenly reached coherence. "You know where we're goin' right now? You're taking me to kill my wife, that cheating cunt!"

Wonderful; he finally learned a new word. Nothing unusual here, another babbling drunk taking his frustra...*Oh, shit!*

"Think I'm fuckin' playing?" As we entered the tunnels, he opened his overcoat. The unmistakable handle of a gun caught my eye. Still, what's he going to do, he'll just sleep it off—I hoped.

"That bitch, she's at my home right now fucking her boyfriend. Hurry up, they're gonna watch each other die tonight!"

I was not altogether convinced. "That's real nice, but how 'bout just keeping that gun in your coat. We'll get there." I veered onto the Banksville exit off ramp.

"Step on it, put the pedal to the medal. You'll get a big tip!"

I drove fast enough to appease him, but I wasn't going to get us both killed. Approaching Crane Avenue, a major intersection, it was evident we could not make the light. I braked to an abrupt stop.

"Run it!" he commanded, in an almost sober tone. I turned around with my *don't fuck with me— I'm a hard-assed cabby face*, momentarily discounting the situation. Out came the gun. He waved it around, with a crazed, wild look, while frantically screaming, "Run the fucking light, go, run it! Run that fuckin' red light!"

My foot never hit a gas pedal faster. I could feel my heart pounding and racing. "Ok, shit, whoa, hey, we'll get there, put that damn gun down!"

The crazy doctor calmed down a tad, placing the weapon next to him on the seat as we high-tailed it out Banksville Road. I'd been doing this job long enough to be keenly aware of the road, especially drunks with cars. However, an infuriated, unhinged drunk with—I assumed—a loaded gun sitting four feet behind the back of my head reached a whole new level. Hey, I know! Maybe it's time to test some of those interactive, crisis intervention skills I had been learning at Penn State.

"Man, Dr. Charlie, I can see the pain you are in, do you want to talk about..."

"Just shut the fuck up and drive! I know what I'm doing!" He scooped the gun up again, this time pointing it barrel down, facing the floor of the cab, twirling it in a slow, circular motion. "They're in for a real fucking surprise!"

I kept driving. Fast. So much for my illustrious people skills. Maybe if I blew through another red light, a Mt. Lebanon cop would light us up and pull us over. Then again, that may not end well either. For an angry, shit-faced, irrational, jealous husband, good solutions were an anomaly.

He was coherent enough by now to provide the necessary lefts and rights toward his impending crime scene, still peppered heavily with his tirade of cussing. I wanted him out of the cab, whatever way possible, but now genuinely felt horrified by the reality of his murderous rant. Though my heart rumbled at a thousand beats per minute, I feared more for the lives of his wife and her "friend" than for my own. I attempted to interject small doses of rationality when he took intermittent breaths between the words kill, fuck, slut, and bitch, but he placed little value on my input.

"Pull over, right over there, at that next corner." Dr. Charlie set the gun on the seat and pulled out his wad of cash. I momentarily entertained the idea of playing hero and grabbing the gun but eradicated the thought. He peeled off two twenties from the money bundle, handing it over the seat. *He may be an asshole—but at least he's an asshole who tips.* What was I thinking, anyway? How far have I devolved?

"Hey, thanks Doc." I decided to give it one last try. "Buddy, come on, are you sure you want to do this?" I grasped at my last available straw.

"Listen, we never met, you don't know me." He held the gun, barrel up, "Understood?" This time, he sounded perfectly clear. Deadly serious.

"Okay." It was the only answer to give, even though we were light years from okay. He opened the door and ran up the cross street, gun in hand, out in the open. I lost sight of him as he cut across the manicured lawn of a white colonial a few houses down, disappearing into the darkness. He obviously did not want me to know where he lived, the crime scene to be.

I sat still for several minutes, shaken, and stunned. Was I about to become an accessory to murder? I contemplated calling in a *Signal Four*, grabbing the microphone and holding it near my mouth for several seconds. What would I even tell the cops? I had no idea where he went. All I did was my job, taking him from point A to point B. I took a deep breath and slowly drove away.

On the way back to town, I stopped at a phone booth and called Dad. Maybe he had a passenger like this one time. He might have even picked up Dr. Charlie; after all, we live in this big time, small town. Dad's advice was to not say anything at this point. If Charlie had committed his crime, the damage was already done. He pointed out that as drunk as Dr. Charlie was, he probably was blowing off steam, and doubted anything would come of this.

I regained my wits, and the rest of the evening was all simply routine. Downright boring. I embraced the mundane like it was the newest love of my life. The next few days, I watched every news channel, scoured both local papers from cover to cover. Nothing notable happened. Nobody shot, murdered, maimed, no one disappeared. After a week, I finally felt licensed to breathe a huge sigh of relief.

I can't say whether I ever crossed paths with Dr. Charlie again. On this job, it's so easy to forget a face. What I'll never forget was this nut-job waving a gun around behind me while I floored the gas pedal through a red light with no hesitation. I suppose the good doctor survived, as well as the slutty wife and her alleged lover. Had I learned otherwise, and the headlines read *Double Murder-Suicide in Docile Suburb*, someone, somewhere would have surely observed: "These things—they always happen in threes!"

CHAPTER 11

Rick Shaw

1979-1980

F red was always right! I kept coming back. Free from
school, free from commitment, free to fuel this strange
addiction.

Fresh out of college, there I was, still driving a taxi.
Was the job market that bad? Not particularly. I chose not
to pursue a low paying, entry-level job in law enforcement
or social services, starting at $18-20K per year in a weak
economy. Hoping to further my formal education down the
road, I rationalized that continuing my informal education
at *Yellow Cab U* easily earned me more money than from any
job I could land at the moment. This would, of course, only be
temporary while I contemplated my next career move.

Temporary somehow morphed into the next five years
as a full- time driver. This was not the actual plan, but life
never follows those premeditated blueprints. After graduation, I moved out of my family home, into an apartment

with a buddy. I lived off my tips, while the weekly paychecks accumulated three or four at a time until I finally got around to banking them. I worked as often, or as little, as I wanted to. It was not a bad situation at all, still loving the freedom and flexibility.

During this period, the taxicab business underwent a complete transformation. In the early 1980's, the cab drivers of Pittsburgh faced intense labor strife as the company promoted the "independent contractor" work concept, transitioning the driver's status from union employee to "at-will lease customer." Most of the drivers, me included, vehemently opposed these changes. Leasing was touted by Yellow Cab under the guise of just an option, but the writing on the wall was inerasable. The local union voted overwhelmingly to strike, and we soon found ourselves on the picket line.

For those with families to support, a strike was an understandable hardship. For me, it was not difficult—rather, a much- needed break. Here it was again—an opportunity to go in a different direction. I was young, a bright future within reach. A real job, a fresh career path, a master's degree?

I thought through the myriad of alternatives and did absolutely nothing to optimize those thoughts. After all, I committed to picket line duty for at least two shifts per week. Being in Pittsburgh, a city with a rich labor tradition, we stood around the flaming steel barrels with pride and solidarity, raising our picket signs as well-wishers honked their horns. And, yes, more than a fair share of people offered single-finger salutes.

While in decent financial shape, I wanted to work at least three days per week. The major hotels and even the airport welcomed the striking cab drivers to serve their respective cab stands in private cars, a perfectly illegal practice commonly known as *jitneying*. A group of us forged our own creative entrepreneurial spirits together, establishing a jitney operation center directly across the street from Yellow Cab. It easily may have qualified as the smallest physical corporate headquarters in the history of the 'burgh--a telephone booth!

Our *marketing department* promptly circulated the phone booth's number to bars, hotels, hospitals, offices, and other steady customers. The business was an instant success! Each of us took turns dispatching, which consisted of hanging around the phone booth fielding calls. For most trips, the phone dispatcher was awarded fifty cents ($1.00 for an airport trip) from the drivers, who signed into a sophisticated queue— a sheet of paper on a clipboard. It was a perfect system, good old-fashioned American ingenuity.

At the time, my personal car was an almost new 1980 Toyota Corolla. It was the first new car I ever owned and had little desire to inhabit it with drunk or stinky passengers, upsetting that unmistakable new car smell. Living in this brave new world of transportation innovation, I made a deal with my friend, Lee, to "lease" his 1974 AMC Matador for jitney purposes. It was the perfect vehicle; generic looking enough to pass for a cab, yet sturdy enough to handle the workload. Something was missing. An identity, perhaps? After countless hours of deep thought and careful consideration, Lee and I decided to nickname the car "Rick Shaw," in honor of, naturally, the *rick-sha*.

Rick served me well for the strike's duration. In retrospect, there was a degree of irony, some definite hypocrisy on my part. Cab drivers have always been less than fond of jitneys and other rogue taxi impersonators, and here we were, doing the same. In my own situation, I walked the picket line for three hours protesting leasing, only to cross the street afterwards to work at the jitney station in my informally leased vehicle.

On occasion, I used my Toyota for special trips. My dad had a healthy client base of steady riders who often went to the airport. When he was unavailable to service those trips, he farmed them out to either a reliable buddy driver or me. While on strike, I ran a few of his steady customers in my own car, including one of Pittsburgh's finest citizens—Mr. Fred Rogers. *Yes, that one!* While it is doubtful that anyone ever embarked on an empirical study of the matter, I am confident I was Mr. Roger's personal jitney driver the only time in his life he ever needed one. With jitneys being illegal, I likely hold the distinct honor of being Mr. Roger's accomplice the only time he ever went astray of the law.

Despite the continued resistance, the strike soon settled. From the start, I maintained that once Yellow Cab got its baby toe in the door, as soon as the first driver signed the company's one-sided lease agreement, it would be the beginning of the end of cab-life as we knew it. The company and the union agreed that all "new hires" (how they could be *hired* if they were not even employees was beyond me) would be lease drivers, while the current drivers had a choice between remaining commission- based employees or becoming "independent contractors" on the company's non-negotiable terms. What became abundantly clear was that in only a matter of time, we would be a glorified car rental agency.

The leasing system, which remains the overwhelming dominant business model for the taxi industry today, is simple in its format. The driver... I mean, the independent contractor leases the cab for a given time- period for a specified price. He/she assumes responsibility for fuel costs, keeping the cab clean, all miscellaneous expenses and any additional fees the company conjures up. All incoming revenue beyond these expenses belongs to the driver. One who knows what they are doing and is willing to hustle has potential to make excellent money. As with any business, however, there are endless risks and few guarantees.

Many of the drivers transitioned to leasing soon after the strike ended. The short- term appeal was easy to understand—a significant pay increase, in the form of cold, hard, daily cash, as opposed to waiting for that deferred and diluted weekly paycheck. As contractors, they were no longer employees. Yellow Cab could no longer tell them when and when not to work, what trips to accept, or what they could or could not do during their shift.

The company, for its part, was delighted with this arrangement, guaranteeing their money regardless of the driver's production or lack thereof. Yellow Cab no longer paid health insurance, vacation, or sick time for the leasers. What many drivers failed to realize was the company's handwashing of any responsibility for workman's compensation insurance, as the drivers were now self-employed. Taxi driving has universally been recognized on countless top-ten lists of most dangerous jobs. The possibility of involvement in a serious accident, combined with the occupational hazard of being easy targets with a pocketful of money easily qualifies cabbies for this distinction. Now classified as independent contractors, should a driver receive the bonus of a concussion from a good, old- fashioned pistol-whipping, or a debilitating injury after a chance meeting with an inebriated driver, the most they could hope for from the company might be a get-well card. Flowers?

Others, including myself, resisted the leasing temptation, out of principle. While our benefits were never on par with government jobs, we recognized the advantage of free health insurance, paid vacation, and, at least in theory, union protection. Although I was always a high booker (revenue producer), I remained among a dwindling number of diehards who refused to make the conversion to leasing. While I would have earned more money leasing, I stubbornly resisted and stood pat. It wound up being an excellent decision to keep my health benefits, as I learned a couple of years down the road when my first child was born.

While there was rarely major animosity between the lease and commissioned drivers, the union visibly weakened. As lease drivers became the majority, they saw no benefit in continuing to pay union dues while receiving no benefits from the company. As the company's long- term plan came to fruition, the number of employee drivers rapidly declined. Within a few years, Chauffer and Taxi Drivers Teamsters Local Number 128 rested in peace—and the gig economy was born.

*Phone Booth/ Jitney Operation
Headquarters*

Photo from 1959 strike. "Yins better honor that picket line!"

CHAPTER 12

JoJo

August 1980

E ven with all four windows cranked open on this sticky
and humid Sunday, the cab's interior remained uncomfortable at best. As I cruised through Downtown, the scant
few folks wandering the streets offered not even a glance in
my direction. With multiple, idled yellow taxis occupying the
cab stands at hotels and bus stations, I contemplated my next
move. The radio was eerily silent. Should I chase the next trip
I hear just to get moving, shift to the airport empty, or go
home and take a break? As I slowed for the red light at Liberty and Sixth Street, the radio's silence broke. "Downtown 2,
Downtown 2."

I noticed the unoccupied Downtown 2 cab stand in front
of Jenkins Arcade, only a short block away. After a half-sec-
ond moral dilemma, I keyed the microphone, "2-6-4."

"2-6-4 on the post?" the dispatcher quizzed, recognizing
it as an unlikely spot for a cab to perch on a lazy Sunday

afternoon. "Okay, 2-6-4, due in ten minutes, 625 Stanwix Street, ring Penthouse 2."

"625, Penthouse 2!" I acknowledged it with a sprig of enthusiasm. I smelled an airport. A time order at a prestigious address satisfies a hungry cab driver with the same intensity as a pack of starving hyenas picking up the scent of a fresh killed wildebeest. And the moral quandary? I was not actually parked at the cab stand, so I "jumped the post." Post jumping is the frowned upon practice of claiming a trip by pretending to be sitting on a call post when you are not. I rationalized my sin away by telling myself, *hey, I was looking right at it.*

The light turned green, and I hustled to stake my claim, easily u-turning on a deserted Stanwix Street to the building's main entrance. Arriving eight minutes early, I shut off the ignition, hit the four-ways and entered the front lobby. The building, known as The Penthouse Apartments, was a twelve-story structure of high-end suites and apartments, the top floor divided into two luxury penthouses. I scanned the call button panel to seek my prey. *Here we go, PH#2- Bradshaw?"*

Holy shit— no, it couldn't be! Terry, the Steelers quarterback, owner of four Super Bowl rings, Bradshaw? I hesitated. There are a lot of people named Bradshaw— yeah, right. I pressed the button.

"Hello?" A young woman's voice echoed through the intercom. I knew it wasn't Terry.

"Uh, Yellow Cab." I offered.

"Could you come up? I need some help."

"Sure, no problem."

She buzzed me in. I hopped on the elevator, lighting up the *PH* button. When I reached the top floor, her apartment's door was open, with three super-sized suitcases awaiting. "Thanks for coming up!" I heard the female voice again, from another room.

"No problem, happy to help." I dragged the first piece to the elevator door, it felt like it weighed more than I did. She obviously was not going on a quick getaway. I turned around... Wow! She was a stunning blonde, stone cold gorgeous! Infectious smile. I was so happy to realize my mini dream of an airport trip; it took more than a minute to comprehend whose luggage I was toting. She was an Olympic figure skater, the girl from the *Cup of Noodles* commercials. Mrs. Terry Bradshaw! I finally put two and two together.

"Hey, you're, are you JoJo Starbuck?" I said as I tasted my foot inside my mouth.

"That's me," she flashed her perfect smile. "And you?"

"Uh...oh, How, uh, Howie." I was starstruck by Miss Starbuck.

We dragged the remaining suitcases to the elevator, down to the awaiting taxi. This was before the day someone produced the brilliant idea to mesh the inventions of luggage and the wheel. It took both of us to lift the largest piece into the Checker's spacious trunk, which easily accommodated her belongings.

After loading the luggage, I opened the rear passenger door for JoJo as I would for any rider. I thought for a second that she wanted to sit upfront but could not navigate the awkward moment. As we set off for The Promised Land, I asked her how Terry was—I knew he was at training camp— but only saw sadness in her eyes. She was leaving him. Leaving here. Not coming back.

As we entered The Fort Pitt Tunnels, I noticed JoJo's arms draping the top of the front passenger's seat. She opted for the jump seat that little kids usually stake claim to, I knew I should have let her ride shotgun! For the next fifteen minutes, each of us found a new friend. JoJo was on her way to California to begin a new life—or resume an old one. She was a spiritual lady, confident of G-d leading her the right way. She asked about my life, my goals, if I were in a relationship. The conversation evolved towards sharing her enthusiastic Christianity, but she respected my boundaries of live and let live Judaism. There was no rush to end the trip upon pulling to the terminal, as we chatted for a couple extra minutes. Yes, this was the soon-to-be ex Mrs. Bradshaw, Olympic champion, and true beauty queen, but that was overshadowed by a sweet, sincere human being.

As we exited the cab, I summoned a skycap—remember those? — to haul her baggage. She joked that I should come to California, ending our mini encounter with a quick hug. I could only wish her the best. She tipped me well, not that it even mattered.

Jump Seats

CHAPTER 13

South Side Story

1968ish

During my *Wonder Years,* Mom and Bubby (i.e., Grand-ma) occasionally dragged me along on their *dahntahn* shopping excursions. Hopscotching between department store bargain basements, discount outlets, and five-and-tens rarely thrilled middle school me. However, the prospect of visiting a lunch counter for the ritual treat of a grilled cheese, French fry, and chocolate milk combo, along with the bus rides—yes, I was a weird kid—made those trips palatable.

The 53F-Express bus stop was a short stroll from our Monitor Street apartment, offering a quick, convenient jaunt to town along the Parkway East. Our homebound ride trav-elled a different routing, using Boulevard of The Allies, a four-laned thruway atop an elevated bluff, shielded only by a short, double-barred steel guiderail perched upon aged, crumbling concrete. The view from the bus window overlooked a deadly drop to the Parkway with a backdrop of the Mon River and the world surrounding its southern shore.

As the bus trudged along the boulevard, I'd stare with awe at the panorama across Monongahela's brown waters, at the so close, yet galaxies away mysterious world called South Side. An orderly, flat city streetscape teeming with row homes, businesses, and warehouses, shadowed by mini mountains of greenery, dotted with an array of modest framed homesteads, skinny roadways, steep stairwells, and scattered church steeples piqued my curiosity. As the view dissipated, dueling smoke spewing steel mills dominated opposite riversides. Classic 1960s Pittsburgh.

Amid this ocean of diverse scenery, what mesmerized me the most was an enormous clock resting above a warehouse roof, illuminated with giant sized neon hands and numerals, alternately flashing the time and this message in bold, gleaming letters—*Have A Duke.* I learned this was the location of The Duquesne Brewery, with the end product's nickname being—your guess! While it would be another twenty years until Dustin Hoffman's brilliant portrayal, I would repeatedly recite the time in a Rain-man like monotone, followed by a louder, upbeat "Have a Duke!" until the clock was out of view. And, sure, my fellow bus riders looked on, wearing expressions ranging from amusement to puzzlement to horror. Even Mom!

Growing up in Pittsburgh, opportunities to satisfy those South Side curiosities were scarce. While it was a literal two-minute trip across a choice of bridges, us *Yinzers* kept to our own safe and familiar sides of the water most of the time.

There was one vivid South Side childhood remembrance for me, on a Christmas Eve in the late sixties. My dad worked as a truck driver for a local company and our family was invited to the South Side Slopes home of one of his work buddies for a holiday celebration. I remember more about the rides there and back than anything about the party itself. As we drove along Carson Street, I was amazed at the endless cluster of modest row houses and small businesses along the way, especially the numerous bars. And even on the night before Christmas, so many were open and crowded, their neon signs welcoming visitors. My empirical conclusion was that the folks on this side of town can get extremely thirsty. Especially on holidays.

***

1982ish

"Downtown ten's open!" blared the Voice of Yellow Cab over the taxi's speaker.

"Two-five-seven! Two-five-seven!" I pleaded into the mic, desperate after getting beat on the last dozen or so calls on a slow Tuesday evening.

"Okay, 257 cab, your lucky night. Get the Victory Bar for Pookie."

My first instinct was to respond with a snark, something like *You're just too kind* or *golly-gee, thanks,* but I caught my breath, sighed, and parroted the order. A downtown dive bar, the Victory was on Smithfield Street near the end of the bridge from South Side. And Pookie? Really? Why can't it be for someone normal? Like Jim. Or Bob. How about Susie?

Of course, I had to double park, jump out and peek my head inside the doorway to summon my trip. "Cab for

Pookie," I announced loud enough to attract the barkeeper's attention. He nodded, turned, and whistled in the direction of a small group gathered at the bar's far end as I retreated to my illegally parked and running vehicle. A great philosopher—I can't recall who or when— once told me, "Don't leave the cab, or it may leave you."

Within two minutes, a man and woman clambered into the back seat. They looked to be in their sixties, but a hunch said they were younger, perhaps worn down by demanding work and life. The familiar scent of cheap booze instantly overtook the taxi.

I turned towards my newfound fare. "Hi; where to?"

The lady spoke first. "Shous-side, up over Barry Street hilltop. We'll show ya."

I threw the flag and drove towards the bridge, disappointed we were not heading east, perhaps to Oakland or Bloomfield where I could work my comfort areas, my safety zones.

Yes, I know, ten years earlier I gazed out a bus window fantasizing about the South Side in the same way normal kids dreamed of Disneyland. Now that I've had my taste, with its narrow streets, alleyways, cobblestones, endless stop signs, red lights, and steep, zig-zagging mazes, South Side was no longer my dream destination.

"Sho, wha's yer name, driver? Where ya from?" asked the gentleman, his yinzer accent eclipsed only by the aroma of whiskey-laden breath. "You a Sau-side boy?"

"Nah, I'm from the city…" I stopped myself, realizing that the South Side's *in* the city. "I mean, you know, I grew up on this side of town. Squirrel Hill, East Liberty, Greenfield. I'm Howie, by the way."

"Hey there, Howdy. I'm (multisyllable, unpronounceable Slovak name beginning with 'P'), but everyone calls me Pookie. And this here's my better half, Ro-Ro."

After crossing the bridge and hanging a left on East Carson, we were greeted by red light after red light. As we approached the intersection of South 17th Street, Ro-Ro poked Pookie, who was half awake. "Hey hon, ain't that Uncle Apples at the bus stop? Probly waitin' on the Ar-leen-ton...hey, Howdy, can you pull over?"

As I obliged, Pookie cranked open his window. "Hey, Apples—ya headed home?"

A portly gentleman wearing thick spectacles and a gray work uniform leaned against a corner sandwich shop, looking left, then right, until finally noticing the yellow beast in front of him. "Hey! Pook! Can yins gimme a lift?"

"Sure; hop in!"

Just my luck, he chose to ride shotgun. As he sat, the entire bench seat sunk, as he was much larger than he appeared at first glance. If he didn't check in at 350 pounds, he must not have weighed an ounce. I readjusted my butt, struggling to see over the steering wheel.

Ro-Ro initiated the South Side formalities. "Uncle Apples, this is our cabby, Howdy."

Uncle Apples offered his hand. "Howdy, Howdy!" Big hand. Memorable grip. "Thanks for stoppin' Pook—just missed that 51A. You know how them things run at night."

I proceeded along Carson Street, now wondering if Uncle Apples was their actual uncle, as he looked ten years younger than Pookie or Ro-Ro... life's unresolved mysteries.

"Hey Howdy," Pookie tapped my shoulder. "Maybe cut up 21st Street, save some lights."

Ro-Ro interjected, "No, go to 26th, it's faster."

Uncle Apples offered up his wisdom; "I'd do 24th if I was you."

I compromised, hitting 23rd, making a left on Mary to Ro-Ro's 26th Street. It seemed to work for everyone.As Ro-Ro guided me through the steep twists and turns of the slopes, Apples and Pookie conversed. "I was dahn the Mill Site Bar earlier," Apples began. "Bad news; Tuba, Sailor, and Stazie are all gettin' laid off next month. Things ain't lookin' good."

They spent the next three minutes reminiscing about the good old days, their changing neighborhood, and things that were no longer around. Ro-Ro directed me up an incredibly steep hill and a sharp-angled left turn, the streets barely wide enough to contain the cab. "Hang this left, we're the one with the yellow awning; Apples is just two doors up."

I stopped, pressing both feet firmly on the brake pedal. Another dime clicked on the meter as we rolled backwards a few inches. Pookie reached over the front seat, passing over two crumpled fives for the $5.50 fare. "The rest is yours. Good ride."

Good tip. "Hey, thanks Mister Pookie! Nice meeting you all."

Uncle Apples reached into his shirt pocket, counting out three one- dollar bills.

"Hey, that's okay; Pookie took care of me," I said, even though I didn't mind.

Apples insisted, "No, that's for you. Beats the shit out-ta takin the damn Arlington bus and walking up 130 city steps!"

Riverfront view of South Side

One of several hundred sets of Pittsburgh city steps

CHAPTER 14

Road Trip

August 16, 1981

The day before, my friend Gary and I set off on a weekend adventure to the South Jersey shore. Our game plan was to meet Kent and Rich, my old college buddies, at Rich's house in Philly, then head to the beach on Saturday morning.

We departed Pittsburgh that Friday morning in my 1980 Toyota Corolla hatchback, navy blue in color with a distinct orange stripe. The road trip was the perfect prescription for a needed respite from taxi life. With Gary embarking on a long, successful writing career, I was two years past graduation, still driving full- time, wondering what to do with my life.

The shore was never a thing for me while growing up. My family didn't have the financial wherewithal to take vacations, although I maintain fond memories of long Sunday drives. And I'd never been a water person, couldn't even swim, yet looked forward to our trip to Wildwood and its blue waters, seashells, sunshine, wild women!

At one point in our car conversation, the sore subject of relationships came up. For the past few years, I vowed to never again commit to a relationship, often reiterating, "I will never get married!" But somewhere along the eastern portion of the Pennsylvania Turnpike, with no forethought, unexpectedly, I blurted this out; "If I met the right girl tomorrow, I would marry her."

While Gary was stunned and bewildered by this out of character statement, I was blown away; I could not believe I said that! I joked that I may have been relapsing from an acid trip but was not sure if I was kidding.

We arrived in Philly, hanging out with Kent and Rich, having a good time, doing Philly type stuff. Whether any cheesesteaks were involved, I can't recall. I'll never forget witnessing gigantic Galapagos tortoise sex at The Philly Zoo. But the meeting the right girl thought drifted far from the oblivion that became my mind.

Saturday morning! The four of us set sail for Wildwood. We decided both Rich and I would drive, as Gary and I planned to stay overnight. Kent and Rich paired up in Rich's mid '70s Plymouth Duster, while Gary and I cruised in the shiny blue Corolla.

Our epic journey began with a stop at a Philly gas station. Rich—well, you must know Rich… great guy, but extreme-ly anal, especially about cars. For the less than two- hour ride, Rich popped open the hood, checking every belt, hose, and obscure fluids most people never realized existed. Kent flashed a smile and rolled his eyes; Kent knew Rich well. I commented about the delay as Rich ensured each tire inflated to *exactly* 32 PSI. Now, I was never a big believer in destiny, but Rich's automotive anal retentiveness changed mine.

Rich led the way, crossing the Ben Franklin Bridge, through South Jersey back roads until we began our south-bound excursion on the Atlantic City Expressway. I began to anticipate a nice day at the beach, away from...

BEEP-BEEP!

Rich and Kent were several hundred feet behind us and that was not the horn of a Plymouth Duster. *Why are they honking, I have the right of way...?*

BEEP!

"Howie, slow down, those girls were honking at us! "

"What are you talking about?"

I looked to my right at a light blue Toyota Celica in the lane next to us. "Yeah, Ree, that's a nice car." At second glance, I discovered three female occupants, featuring an alluring driver with long blonde hair, smiling and waving. Their beeps were enthusiastically reciprocated.

Gary opened his window, and somehow, through the wind and road noise, concluded that they, too, were Wildwood bound. To this day, Gary remains a great communicator.

For the next 45 minutes, we continued down the road-way, occasionally passing each other. Rich and Kent followed along, trying to decipher the dancing Toyotas in front of them. After empirical scientific research, we deduced they could be college students. I kept driving. Gary had the better view.

"Hey man, I get the driver!" I said half joking, half staking a claim.

"No," countered Gary, "I get the driver, I saw her first!"

"It doesn't work that way. I get her cause we're both driving blue Toyotas on the same highway!"

Gary played along. "Sorry, she's with me."

At this point, it was time to stand up for myself. "No, I get the driver, *YOU* can have the little sister in the back seat!"

We had no idea where this would go but went with the flow. Upon arriving in Wildwood, we met three alluring, statuesque blondes. There was Debbie, the delectable driver, Diane, the pretty shotgun passenger, and the cute" little sister" in the back seat, Chris. We had a nice group to spend a day with and headed to the beach and boardwalk.

Although we had valiantly fought for dibs on Debbie, it was Chris who I spent the most time with. In the inevitable course of group small talk, the "what do you do when you're not on the beach" question surfaced. Rather than simply stating our current career paths, we played a game where we described our jobs. Gary, a music journalist, and Kent, a funeral director, had impressive and interesting descriptions. It was now my turn to try to make it at least look like I had a real job.

After an extensive monologue about being a key player within a major corporation who makes his own hours, drives a company car, escorts beautiful women around town, and meets big executives at the airport, while people throw money at me as all this is happening, Diane and Debbie looked perplexed as Chris easily solved the mystery; "Cab Driver!"

When the rest of the group made the inevitable trek to the ocean, I was having enough fun to join them, even though I had no clue about surviving in the water. As I waddled deeper into the heavy waves, trying to impress the girls with dirty jokes, the water began getting the better of me. I heard Rich yell, "Hey, Howie, be careful—you know you can't swim!" He was right. I reluctantly retreated, feeling like the fifth—seventh? –wheel, the odd one out.

I retreated to our beach spot, settling down to enjoy the sights and sounds of Wildwood. When the rest of the group exited the water, beach location amnesia overtook them. No form of GPS existed in 1981, so Rich concocted a brilliant idea to reconnect with me. He attempted to flap his hands in a way that I uniquely did, producing an odd snapping sound combining rapid contact with the fingertips and palms of my hands. He explained to everyone that if they could do this— up to then, only I had this ability—that I would take notice. Naturally, Rich could not come close to imitating the motion or the sound. Chris looked at him nonchalantly, magically choreographing both the freaky motion and sound. "You mean like this?"

It was too much. Kent, usually mild mannered and reserved, grabbed Chris by her arm, leading her across the beach searching for me. Upon our reunification, Kent, looking as if he had just discovered The Beatles, excitingly pointed out the similarities of Chris's and my own hand flapping (talent?).

The rest of the day consisted of innocent light fun. It was a great day, but as we walked the lovely ladies to their car at sunset, I realized we would probably never see them again.

However, just before they drove off, Chris suggested that we all exchange addresses and keep in touch. Somehow, a pen and some paper appeared, and information was exchanged by all. I thought sarcastically, "Yeah, ok, this is going to happen."

Rich and Kent took off about an hour later. It was great seeing them again. The rest of the evening, I could not stop thinking about the sweet, beautiful women we spent the day with, while saddened by the reality that we would unlikely cross paths again.

I glanced at the addresses. They were from Woodbury, N.J., wherever that was. On the way home that Sunday morning, we indeed passed an exit marked *Woodbury*. I told Gary how I wished we could get off and find our newly found friends. What a dumb idea!

I returned home, back to cabbing; the mini vacation buried in the back of my mind. The next week, I opened my mailbox and there it was—a letter postmarked Woodbury N.J. It was from Chris! Although she was seeing someone else at the time—I would *never* intrude—we became pen pals. After two months of intense letter writing—*E-mails or Facebook will never hold a candle to great hand- written letters*— we finally spoke on the phone. The first call lasted four hours!

Fast forward to August 21st, 1982, one year and five days after our initial—was it just a chance? – encounter. I find myself at a wedding reception. Gary, one of the groomsmen retells a story in an entertaining and elegant manner. I cannot recall any of the details except for this one: "...and he ended up marrying that little sister in the back seat..."

The Wildwood Seven:
From left to right-Front row: Diane, Debbie, and
Chris. Second row: Rich, Kent, Gary, and Howie

CHAPTER 15

Radio Days

Before My Time thru 1998

Dateline 1998:
   I resist. Always stubborn to embrace the latest techno-fad. Twenty years from now, I will cling to a yet to be invented, but by then obsolete flip-phone. And I continue composing with a basic Bic pen in spiral, college ruled notebooks.

Resistance surrenders to resignation, a begrudging acceptance. The clear choices are to go with the program or abandon ship. Yellow Cab decided to implement their next new shiny object. A computerized dispatch system displaced the two-way radio.

It took some time, but conformity was the sole alternative. The taxi world was now my only bread and butter. The static laced voice box and microphone were replaced by a small screen with zone numbers and printed messages. More than one hundred zones encompassing specified geographic boundaries, replaced the radio call posts. We had the option to log into (or not) any zone of our preference and be placed into a queue within the area. When fares became available in that zone, the computer automatically assigned it to the first cab up. If no cabs were booked within a zone, the open trip appeared on the screen, ready to be claimed by the fastest fingers.

On the surface, it was a fair way to distribute fares. The dispatchers maintained their job security by adjusting to a new role of monitoring the system and matchmaking cab requests into appropriate zones. A red panic button on the bottom of the keypad supplanted the emergency signal-four help call. A two- way radio remained under the dashboard, with the caveat of being seldom used. The new protocol was to press a key marked *Voice* and await permission for an audience with the dispatching pope du jour. If the dispatcher wanted to talk to a specific driver, he would send a *Go Voice* private message.

Of course, with the invention of cell phones, time- honored traditions of dispatchers tipping off their buddies persevered, albeit even more under the radar. On the bright side, the drivers were free to crank up their favorite tunes in lieu of the all- night talk shows of grizzled, rambling voices muttering addresses. Many drivers carried aspirin or much stronger remedies to fight that phenomenon. However, staring at an eight by ten- inch screen littered with numbers for hours on end made me sometimes yearn for an aspirin, or three, and strangely miss the humanity behind those voices.

***

It seemed that taxicab radio banter had been around since the dawn of time. I recall the rare occasions riding in taxis as a kid (loved those jump-seats!), wondering where the voice in the box came from and what was with that gibberish? I guessed *Dahntahn 7 – 'Sliberdy 6-Shady 2- Etner- Mahnoliver-Car-nayg-ie- and Mickees-Rox* to be some local offshoot of English, but nothing I ever heard outside of the confines of a cab.

Most radio dispatch systems such as police, fire, or public utilities operated within a singular frequency, with all sides of a conversation easily monitored on any scanner. In cabs, only the dispatchers' voices were audible, as the drivers' transmissions occupied a separate frequency. The dispatchers usually wore headsets, but sometimes broadcast with an open microphone, allowing sporadic bits and pieces from the drivers' airwaves to be transmitted. The company's preference was to minimize the chatter.

The studio for this 24/7 talk radio show was called "the exchange," located above the garage. There were several call takers, usually women, who fielded orders and complaints from the riding public. They were joined by up to three on duty dispatchers, depending upon the time and day. Until the 1990s, all the dispatchers were male. I suppose one could label the company as sexist, but this was far from atypical of workplace cultures of those days.

While the job could become monotonous, the radio could be downright entertaining. Each dispatcher brought their distinctive voice and radio persona to the table, often imitated by groups of drivers counting out time at the airport.

Sometimes I would get a laugh from listening to dispatchers arguing with other drivers. Although I heard one side of the conversation, it wasn't hard to imagine the verbiage of the combative drivers. Or hearing the frustrations of dispatchers trying to give directions to clueless drivers—we do have a complex little city. One dispatcher famously instructed those who were not getting it, "No, look at me!" At least I found it funny.

For we who made their living off radio calls—there were many who have always fared quite well without them—listening skills were imperative. Translating the mumbo-jumbo cackling heard over the cabs' speakers depended upon our abilities to analyze and dissect the idiosyncrasies of each individual dispatcher. If fishing for an airport trip, the subtlest hint might be all we needed. Sometimes it was simple—an emphasis on a syllable, a change in tone. Even a pause. The dispatcher's goal was to "clean the board," to get all the trips covered. There often were more fares than willing takers. One dispatcher would resort to games like *Pick-a Port,* or *Needle in the Haystack,* with one or two airports, or long trips hidden within a cluster of open calls. The object was to pick the winner for the driver and clean up the board for the dispatcher. And it usually worked well.

When business was slow, the dispatcher's job was easy. Every open trip elicited heavy competition. The only negative was the inevitable headache from hearing ten desperate cab drivers screaming in his ear for the opportunity to chauffeur Ms. McGillicutty to her hair appointment. Often, there were more fares to be had than drivers bidding on them, and it became game time.

For example, there is a board full of open trips and I am fishing for an airport trip. My watch reads 1:43 PM. The dispatcher offers a word salad of options. "Okay, we have Uptown 2, Soho1, Oakland 2,4, &7, Shady- 3, Squirrel Hill 3 and 5, Edgewood, Forest Hills, South Side 4, Brentwood, Mt Lebanon 1 &4, Elliot, and Emsworth open. Who's where?"

I just dropped off in Point Breeze, so Shadyside, Squirrel Hill, and Edgewood are close. The logical choice is to take one of those calls—but I'm in cherry-picking mode. I grasp the mic, finger ready on the button, awaiting the dispatcher to make his move.

He drops his first clue. "Who's around Mt Lebanon 4?" That's kind of far for me, but before I can even get to "maybe," a quick- witted driver jumps all over it. A street address in a tony area is given. It sounds even more airport-y to me as the dispatcher adds: "Due at 2 PM."

The mic remains in hand. I recall the Mt Lebanon 4 was offered three minutes earlier, at 1:40, followed by a Forest Hills. And I know that this dispatcher consistently calls out suburban time orders twenty minutes before their requested pick- up time, and, that a sizable percentage of these pre-scheduled trips are airports. Before the dispatcher barely pronounces the "For" in Forest Hills, I am all over it. "One-five-two, one-five two, one-five-two!" My adrenaline gets the better of me.

"Okay, jeez, one-five-two, calm down! WTAE for..."

And, fifteen minutes later, I find myself loading the luggage of a local reporter from the television station. My good fortune.

Each dispatcher had their subtle and not so subtle ways to advertise trips. When flooded with an ocean full of fares Downtown, he might simply advertise, "How 'bout Downtown 13 at The Westinghouse Building?" An astute cabby follows the scent, happily meeting up with a pair of suits toting briefcases ready for their flight home after a grueling workday. Other trips may be sold using color commentary. "Going east." "Heading west." "Aspinwall has wings!" (Airport.) "Decent." (*Better* than decent.) "Hazelwood for a Choo-choo!" (Railroad crew.) "Greentree One for The Promised Land." (Definite airport.) "Who wants to go for a ride?" (Better have at least a couple of hours available.) And, my favorite, the champion of Yellow Cab jargon, "Not a bad trip!"

While it was a known fact that many of the dispatchers played favorites, and got paid off, some were straight shooters. One of the best was Johnny, whose last name was a perfect match for a famous label of whiskey. Mr. Walker was among the more competent and professional members of Yellow Cab's radio corp. He had the most clear and concise voice I have ever heard over any broadcast medium, superior to any newscaster or mellow FM radio disc jockey. He went through phases where he would intentionally comment in clichés or be overpolite on the air. "I beg your pardon, sir," or, "that's like being a day late and a dollar short." This was his way to break up monotony; or inject a little humor into an often stressful job. His as well as ours.

The dispatchers were cognizant of the work routines of individual drivers. The sad and plain truth was that there were cab drivers who refused trips to certain areas, some out of fear, others out of ignorance. The dispatchers who knew these drivers either ignored them if they were bidding a trip to "a bad area," or simply told them, "It's not for you." Discrimination has always been a legitimate stain on the reputation of the taxi industry.

Other drivers were creatures of habit. Many worked exclusively between Downtown and The Promised Land, taking few, if any radio trips. There were those I labeled "Eds and Meds Drivers" who concentrated in and around Oakland, known for its renowned universities and phenomenal medical centers. Others favored their personal corners of the world. There was an elderly gentleman called "Lunch Buckets" whose nightly forte included ferrying local bargoers to their humble abodes in the hills straddling the North Side. For years, "Hilton Bob" migrated to the feeder line on the hotel cab stand, no matter what else was happening around town. Even when The Hilton was rebranded under the Wyndham umbrella, he remained Hilton Bob. There was a man I didn't know by name, Cab#401, who staked his claim around the Ohio Valley, patrolling either side of the Ohio River. He roamed neighborhoods like Woods Run, Bellevue, Avalon, and McKees Rocks—or in cab lingo—*The Rocks.* Yellow had numerous contract trips from trucking companies in *the bottoms,* an industrial area below the McKees Rocks Bridge. The truckers were provided with taxi vouchers for the trip across the Ohio to The Avalon Motel, quick and easy, minimal risk rides. Cab #401 made his living shuttling those truckers along with other locals in his neck of the woods.

Another territorial specialist was "Penn Hills Harry." Pittsburgh's largest and most diverse suburb, Penn Hills borders the city and Wilkinsburg to the west, and Plum, another municipality of ample square mileage, to its east. Harry made a significant percentage of his living in these areas. Dispatchers respected that, favoring him on those calls, knowing he would never get lost, or blow off an order. Harry ruled the burgh's far east.

Me? I had no favorite niche. I tended to work in the inter-city neighborhoods, between the rivers, but was never afraid to venture around the county. Sometimes I raided Mr. Bucket's northern turf, or, ended up in and worked "The Rocks." While there was plenty to go around, I was never angry when creatures of habit were given first dibs within their unofficial turf.

One of the most eccentric cabbies was a gentleman owning the nickname "Aggie." Imagine yourself on a dream vacation in Venice, Italy. You hire a gondolier. Only one minor problem: Your gondola driver stipulates that he will not travel underneath the hundreds of bridges lining the canals. Perhaps you have just met a cousin of our own Aggie.

Here in the city with the most bridges in the Western Hemisphere (Venice rules the other side), the city trisected by three major rivers, lived a cabby who would not cross a bridge over water, troubled or not. Aggie had a sincere phobia of bridges. He would cross the smaller spans or overpasses between the rivers, yet would not venture to the northern, southern, or western reaches of the city. Although there were no applicable ADA laws in the eighties, the dispatchers understood Aggie's plight and did their best to accommodate him. Hungry drivers knew when Aggie was working and heard the dispatcher say, "No, Aggie, this one's not up your alley," insinuating that the fare included crossing a river at some point, perhaps even leading to The Promised Land.

Understanding the 'burgh, a city with a complex geography of spaghetti woven streets and roadways was a challenge for those on either end of the radio. GPS, not even *Map Quest* were concepts. Many of the dispatchers were ex-cabbies who knew the region but could consult a map when needed. Even paper maps were not always dependable, as they showed "paper streets" which were nothing more than undrivable paths, walkways, or steep city steps, reconnecting with another block of a street sharing its name. The informative dispatchers would let us know when these obstructions emerged, pinpointing the locations. "Beechview on Belasco, the part off Hampshire... South Side 3 up Billy Buck Hill... South Side 4 on Mary, down The Hollow... Stanton Heights on New Camelia... Squirrel Hill 5 on Shady Extension." We are a city with innumerable quirks, familiar only to local yokels and taxi people.

The operators, drivers, and dispatchers knew the regulars, those steady reliable customers who depended on us. From the cabbies' viewpoints, while these trips did not always translate into big money, we respected their value to our business. The dispatchers often advertised the trips by passenger's names; need one for Stella, Lawrenceville 2... Greenfield for Cowboy at Big Jim's. Or they would preface the street name using *"The"* as a definer. For a random rider in Garfield on Jordan Way, they simply said, "cab on Jordan Way." But for the lady who rode to work every day at 4 AM, it was Garfield for *The* Jordan Way. We would gladly grab the quick trip in Bloomfield for *The* Winebiddle... Sheraden for

The Huxley... Perrysville for *The* Osgood... Carrick for *The* Hazeldell... Larimer for *The* Shetland. These trips were easy sells—steady riders going to and from work won the hearts of hard- working cab drivers. In this profession, where any given trip could instantly turn tragic, those dependable regulars provided a sense of security.

As fascinating as the radio world was, it was equally frustrating. The blatant favoritism by dispatchers towards their friends was hard to ignore. There were ways to combat it. When it was slow, some of us drivers who "were out of the loop" headed to high ground, or "sweet spots." Yellow Cab's radio tower was located on Mount Troy across the northern border of the city. I learned that by parking in open high spots perpendicular to a place where the tower was visible, you can drown out competition in lower lying locations. Some of the best places were the Hill District's Sugartop neighborhood, and Fineview, a mountainous section of North Side. Grandview Avenue, overlooking the city from Mount Washington, was another sweet spot. The dispatchers didn't appreciate us blowing their buddies off the air, but it sure helped level the playing field.

One thing about me is I have never been one to hide my opinions. This backfired during the radio era of the early eighties. I became an outspoken critic of the unfairness and favoritism by the dispatchers, especially after many drivers converted into independent lease contractors. As a company driver, I was still only paid 45% of the fares, while the leasers received 100% of their take, minus expenses. With leasing alive and thriving, the drivers had more incentive to slip the dispatchers a fiver or a ten spot here and there when they were "helped" with a big trip. I did not believe in paying off dispatchers. My open critiques soon landed me on the "shit-lists" of several dispatchers. And there was little I could do about it. I was among a minority of drivers still paying union dues, but filing a grievance was a useless endeavor, as all the union officers were in the loop.

To compound the situation, Yellow Cab aggressively re-cruited leasers, putting more drivers on the road than ever in an economically struggling market. There was less and less to go around; I fought for whatever crumbs I could get. Things were rough, our steel industry was in freefall. I began hating a job I once loved. I shortened my workdays, taking on a sec-ond job, ironically, as a radio dispatcher for AAA. Cabbies were being attacked and robbed at alarming rates, many of these incidents violent. Hostilities formed between lease and commission drivers, even between leasers and other leasers. There was frustration, everyone wanted their slice of an ever -shrinking pie. Drivers were angry with the company. And tired of the inequity over the radio.

***

On a routine Saturday afternoon on January 30,1982, some-one at Yellow Cab became a statistic. Shot at point blank in the head by a man with a mask while simply doing his job. Maybe it was an inevitable part of the profession, the cab business is indeed high risk.

It was not a cabby killed that day. It was a dispatcher. A man walked into Yellow Cab's exchange, where two dis-patchers and several operators were at work, and fired in cold blood. The victim, Jim Sweeney, carried a reputation as one of the good guys. I never knew him well, met him in passing once or twice. Why would anyone murder this man?

The case was never solved; justice was not served. There were whispers that the killer had mistakenly shot the wrong man, the intended target being his co-worker. One rumor floated about a gambling debt. Years later, one driver told me he was confident it was a vengeful cabby who was still active but would not divulge his suspect. Hopefully, one day we will learn the truth.

Two-way dispatch radio

The dispatch screen replaced the two-way radio.

CHAPTER 16

Wilkinsburg Bandit

October 1983

I t's 4:40 AM. On the road again! Is this it? Is this as good as it gets; will this be my life's work?

I recently switched to working daylight, but missed the night shifts, where I knew the routines. It was easier to read street life in the night than in sunshine. Turning in at three or four in the morning beat the hell out of starting at four AM.

Although I'd been working these shifts for a few months, I never comfortably adapted to the life of a morning and afternoon cabby. Compounding that, our region was engulfed in a severe economic downturn as factories closed and neighborhoods deteriorated. More taxis filled the streets than I ever remembered, as laid-off workers filtered into whatever means were available to make ends meet. The volume of taxi business steadily declined as financially strapped families scratched cab rides from their to-do lists. Pookie and Ro-Ro still visited their South Side watering holes, but would forego the last shot, nurse their beers, and climb steep city steps to their humble slope-side homes rather than shell out that three-dollar cab fare.

Competing with more dogs for less meat wouldn't have bothered me had the competition been fair. The dispatchers had their favorites who were hand-fed the treats while the rest of us fought for scraps. Two of the morning dispatchers had me on their unofficial shit lists, one because I previously called him out regarding his radio favoritism. The other disliked my father, and extended that to me, although I never recalled having a single one-on-one interaction with the guy. But it was what it was, my only recourse being to take whatever I could get.

"Wilkinsburg-3, *Wilky 3*," muttered my obnoxious radio nemesis. Pause. "Wilkinsburg 3, open."

Oh, what the hell, no one's going to fight me for this. "One-five-two, one-five-two!" I half-heartedly pleaded my case.

"Okay, 1-5-2, all yours; Come over to 412 South Trenton."

"412 Trenton, roger that." I pulled away from the Centre Avenue garage. What did I have to lose? It was probably a shitty little trip, but at least an icebreaker. I knew the call was mine the moment I reached for the mic because drivers were heavily avoiding Wilkinsburg in recent weeks due to a one-man crime wave. A few weeks before, my wife and I and our newborn son settled into our first home, a modest row-house on Wilkinsburg's Ramsey Street—I should provide service to my new hometown! And it was only a couple of weeks prior, at five in the morning, when I grabbed a *Wilkinsburg- 2* order which intrigued no one else. Pasadena Street turned out to be a sweet ride to The Promised Land, topped off with a cherry of a good tip. On this job, unpredictability at times transforms into the gourmet dessert of a fine feast.

The obvious dangers of the job are the other side of that unpredictability. The 1980s were a rough period for Pittsburgh's cabbies, with our recession fueling a substantial heroin epidemic. There was a recent rash of robberies throughout the city, but one single culprit stood out.

The Wilkinsburg Bandit wreaked havoc upon the area where the city's Homewood neighborhood and Wilkinsburg intersect. Up to this point, he robbed around a dozen drivers over a period of three months. His mode of operation was predictable, simple. He walked over to popular downtown cabstands, usually near a hotel, or the Greyhound, and rode to darkened side streets in Homewood or Wilkinsburg. Once there, the weapon, a .38 caliber pistol was presented, along with an unsubtle, unapologetic request for 'the money, all of it!' Word spread as he became bolder and more aggressive, pressing the gun against the head of at least two of his victims. His latest prey was pistol-whipped to the point of spending two nights in the hospital. These robberies occurred between 10 PM and 3 AM, usually originating from downtown.

The description varied slightly from incident to incident, but all depicted a tall, lanky dark-skinned Black male in his thirties, a good six foot two or three, with closely cropped hair and scruffy facial growth. One of his earlier victims, an elderly African American driver, told me he stared the entire trip with a crazed, paranoid look before directing him into a remote alley, punctuating his *gimme all your money* demand with the N-word. The Wilkinsburg Bandit was an equal opportunity criminal—the only color he valued was green.

It was only a six- minute drive to the South Trenton address. Sure, it was Wilkinsburg, but I wasn't concerned. This was at a private home in a not too bad part of the borough. The bandit practiced his medicine mostly from Downtown taxi stands. And it was almost five o'clock, well past his bedtime. I drove along Penn Avenue, passing the all-night gas station straddling the city- Wilkinsburg line, taking temporary comfort at the sight of two Wilkinsburg and a single Pittsburgh police unit parked in the lot, as they frequently do. Two blocks east, I turned right on Trenton, driving the three short blocks into the four hundred numbers. "Why can't these idiots turn on some lights, so I know where to stop?" I wondered while aiming the spotlight manually with my left hand to where I thought *412* should be. No sign of life...

A shadow bolted between two parked cars, the back door opened, slammed shut, all within two seconds, he was in! It only took one glance to realize I rolled the wrong dice. I knew what this was.

"We're goin' to Meade Street, behind Penn Avenue, my man." He could have at least wished me a good morning!

Meade Street is in North Point Breeze, a neighborhood bordering Homewood. Real estate people referred to the area as Point Breeze North, while skeptics dismissed it as Homewood South. It was less than a single mile ride, quite walkable at any time of day. Why not now?

I strategized as I hit the red light at Penn Avenue. *Okay; when this light changes, I'll make my left, then pull into the well-lit Sunoco oasis ahead, hit my high beams, blast the horn, and the cops will rescue me from this situation.*

The light changed, I turned, my heart racing as I neared the – *Shit, they're gone!* The one time I need the police is the only time they're not here. I continued down Penn. "Sir, which part of Meade do you want to go?" I asked, attempting to mask my anxiety with civility.

"Just keep drivin', I'll tell ya— there—the next one, yeah, make the right."

I turned on North Lex, then he directed me to hang the right onto Meade Street. This block was nonresidential, consisting of darkened warehouses and parking lots.

"Yo, pull over, by that building!"

I stopped the cab, smiling nervously. "Hey man, this one's on the house. It was so easy I'd feel bad charging you for it, go ahead." I am a terrible liar.

He was all business. No gun. "You know what this is— you know the deal; all your money, your wallet." Out it came, the razor blade, a super-sized box slicer. He wrapped his left arm in a chokehold around my neck, his unsteady right hand teasing the razor to my exposed right side. "I ain't playin' boy!"

I was frozen, stunned. Terrified would be an understatement. I raised both arms as he pulled the blade slightly away. "Okay, okay, get that thing outta my face, I'll get you the fuckin' money!" He loosened his grip, still holding the blade, sweating, his hand shaking. His level of desperation was obvious, a drug addict willing to do whatever it took. I prayed for my donation to suffice.

"I just started my shift—this is all I got." I said, handing over my fifteen bucks.

"What the fuck? You got more than that; gimme that fuckin' wallet!"

"I just started, it's all I have, I swear to G-d." I opened my empty wallet.

He snatched it away, pocketing my few bucks in his pants while putting the wallet and menacing blade into his coat pocket.

I pleaded, "Hey, can you at least give me my license and ID back? They are useless to you." I had no credit cards.

"Fuck you, *mothahfucka*—you wasted my time!" My buddy from work was right, he did have crazy eyes. The door opened and he fled behind the cab.

I punched it into reverse, the door still open, and pounded the gas pedal, barely missing my moving target as he bolted to the sidewalk, vanishing into a narrow walkway between two buildings. He was history.

Yes, I wanted to run him down with the cab! Had I succeeded, I may have slowly run over him another time as he reeled in pain. Like a steam roller. But it was not going to be. The Wilkinsburg Bandit struck again.

I was angrier at myself than happy to have survived the ordeal. I wished he'd at least pulled the gun instead of that fucking boxcutter. A quick bullet to the head would be preferable to a deadly, arterial slow bleed from a razor —just saying.

I decided against picking up the microphone and calling in a signal four. I did not want to reward the jag-off dispatcher on the other end with the last laugh. I drove to the East Liberty Police Station to report the robbery.

The lieutenant at the station was familiar with the man and said that he needed to be caught before someone was killed. He was also suspected in several bank and small business robberies in the same area.

Later that day, I went to the Penn Dot offices, paid for a new copy of my driver's license, and returned to work the next day. Over the next few weeks, I only heard of one more robbery of a driver involving the Wilkinsburg Bandit. He went back to his downtown, late night routine, returning to his standard gun operational mode. For whatever reason, I was the only one I heard of who enjoyed the box-cutter treatment.

The ordeal soon enough exited my thoughts. Not that I would forget him entirely, but the aftershock was short lived. These things happen to drivers if they stick around long enough, it's part of the job. Around four months later, he resurfaced, the lead story on the six o'clock news.

In addition to robbing numerous cab drivers, he was the prime suspect in a rash of bank robberies. I suppose he graduated, upgraded to bigger money. Police apprehended him at a vacant building on Stanton Avenue in East Liberty, which doubled as a shooting gallery for the addicted. During his arrest, the police chased him up a fire escape connected to the building. The Wilkinsburg Bandit would not be taken easily, throwing a police officer down the metal steps, severely injuring her.

I was never summoned to testify—my fifteen bucks wouldn't have made a dent. I suppose positive identification in multiple bank hold-ups and assault on a police officer was enough to put him away for a long time. The Wilkinsburg Bandit would not strike again.

CHAPTER 17

RSVP: Regrets Only

1984

Would haves; could haves; should haves…if only I did this rather than that, what if I'd taken some other path? Why didn't I listen or speak out? All of us harbor such reflections, regrets, and self-doubts.

Cabbing turned out to be a great gig to work my way through school. A university degree was the sure ticket to better myself, a way to avoid the financial hardships my family endured throughout my youth. I wanted that degree without crippling debt and Yellow Cab enabled me to realize that goal.

I completed my academic studies in May1979 but never even bothered to attend my own commencement ceremonies, a definite should have. Some local event, which I could not even begin to remember anything about, signaled a big money-making weekend for cabbies, and I was not about to pass up those potential big bucks! I rationalized how it was not worth a three- hour ride, hotel rooms, and wearing a suit to be handed a piece of paper, even for this once-in-a-life-time achievement. My parents were upset with my decision, as it would have been a big deal for them to watch the first Ehrlichman be formally summoned and handed a college diploma, but I allowed greed to get the better of me. I assured them that it was "no big thing, not worth the trip."

I look back, recalling nothing special about playing cab driver that weekend. If only I had a time machine, I would have gone to satisfy my parents. I should have gone for *myself*. Perhaps experiencing all the pomp and circumstance could have motivated me to move in an entirely different direction. It was not until the end stages of my parents' lives some thirty years later that I was able to comprehend the depth of my regret for not fulfilling what I deemed at the time to be an insignificant ritual.

No longer another kid working his way through college, I was a true cabbie, a full-time hack with a fancy degree. I was not alone—there have always been well educated people driving taxicabs. The plan became to do this for "a little while," put away some cash, and postpone real life until a later date.

Life refused to go with the program. Shortly after graduation, I rented an apartment with a good buddy. Two years later, met the girl of my dreams. The following year, marriage. Ten months later, parenthood. Next a mortgage. Life would not wait for me to make up my mind. I cheered on my friends as they moved onward and upward in their careers, while parking my butt in the drivers' seats of yellow Checkers night after night, day after day…and year after year. I never abhorred the taxi business; it always intrigued me, but I despised myself for failing to move forward.

Sure, I took baby steps along the way. I would update my resume from time to time, but there was not much to add. I tested for three police officer jobs, one of which I became a finalist for. I removed myself from contention, however, when we committed to our first house in Wilkinsburg, exceeding the boundaries of the ten-mile aerial radius needed to meet that department's civil service requirements. It was probably for the best, as I may have shot someone—especially if they had robbed a hard-working cab driver.

I took a side job as a radio dispatcher for AAA Emergency Road Services. Working daylight shifts on the cab, neither my commissions nor tips measured up to the success I had as a night driver. Triple A was decent money for a part time job. I worked Saturday mornings and a couple 3 -11PM shifts during the week after turning in my cab. It provided much needed extra income and a refreshing diversion from cab life. My regional geographic expertise enabled me to excel, rarely needing to rely on wall maps to match calls to the appropriate units. I enjoyed the relationships developed through the banter with the service and tow truck drivers over the radio, often injecting my warped sense of humor into the mix. AAA offered me a full- time position after a few months, but I did not see it as a career option, electing to work on a part time, as needed basis.

Five years after college, I continued my foray inside the taxi world. I was just a cab driver, transporting the movers and shakers of the world while going nowhere in my own life. They never had to say it. It was a look in their eyes, the tones of their voices, their facial expressions were all it took. Some passengers verbalized it— "You're nothing but a fuckin' cab driver!" or some similar sentiment. I can't deny how often I looked in the mirror, arriving at the same conclusion. I felt hopeless, like a passenger with no specific destination on a meandering commuter train, bearing the head-sign— *NO-WHERE EXPRESS*. I was just a cab driver in a rust-belt town, nothing more.

My wife, Chris, always 100% supportive, believed in me more than I had ever believed in myself. She suffered through my obnoxious babble of could haves and what ifs. I wallowed in self-doubt. I could have gone to graduate school, why didn't I major in business? Journalism? Maybe I should have said yes to AAA, could have earned a promotion by now. Was college a waste of time and money?

We often discussed these options and missed opportunities. While attending Penn State's local campus, I continued working at Ross' Fruit Market, where I started at age sixteen. Although I was hired as a delivery boy/gopher, I evolved into a jack-of-all-trades for the business. Lou Ross, the owner, was at the point where he wanted to retire and sell his business, hoping to see it persevere. I was surprised when he offered me first dibs. He proposed the idea of my father, who had experience in produce years prior, and me buying his store at a below market price—Mr. Ross still owned the building— which he would finance at practically no interest.

I understood the generosity of the offer but had zero interest in a career in fruits and vegetables, let alone any type of business venture. The answer was a basic, "I'm flattered, but no thanks."

What an opportunity to pass over! An established business (since 1951) on an excellent corner in Squirrel Hill, Pittsburgh's most diverse, populated, and viable neighborhood. The truth? Dad and I would probably not see eye to eye, and at eighteen, I was too young and naïve for such a level of responsibility.

The business was sold to a guy named "Speedy"—yes, really—who I continued working for until leaving for State College the following year. Speedy renamed the business *The Greengrocer*. I helped him transition into a complex business he knew little about. Over the next several years, Speedy and I remained on good terms as he changed and grew his business, while I sometimes looked back and wondered "what if?"

As the years went by, I only popped by The Greengrocer on rare occasions to say hello or buy some strawberries. The year was 1984. I was not concerned about whether Big Brother was watching, but one thing was for sure—I was 26 years old with a family and little hope for the future. I was just a cab driver. I had to do something else. Anything else—but what?

CHAPTER 18

Speedy Bump

May 1984

It began a typical morning, the combination of my indecision, bad decisions, bad luck, and perpetual top-ten status on the dispatchers' shit- list not helping the cause. Now five light years removed from my college non-graduation, this was my world.

I pulled out of the cab yard about five in the morning, grasping for any icebreaker I could get. As usual, the sound of my voice barking *one-five-two* was intentionally inaudible to the overnight dispatcher. After an hour of countless strike-outs, I secured a trip from Garfield. An area with a reputation for crime and blight, taxi requests in Garfield seldom yielded heavy competition. Well, at least it was something.

The ride was a short one, a ten-minute jaunt to *Howard Johnson's Motor Lodge* in South Oakland. My passenger, a stocky, bearded African American man pushing fifty, spent the entire trip bitching how he had tried to call a cab three separate times since 4 AM and how sick he was of "you white motherfuckers in cabs" blowing him off. It was useless to point out that many of our drivers were nonwhite, and he was not about to entertain the *Hey, at least I took your call and showed up* routine. The rant continued and I was not about to stop him. A good cab driver is at his best a good listener. I heard him—he had a point. Finding cabs in neighborhoods like Garfield in 1980's Pittsburgh was a dicey proposition.

The hotel's main entrance was on the side- lower level of the building, with an attached "Ho-Jo's" restaurant occupying the upper level, with an independent entrance and parking lot. As my passenger tossed his fare on the front seat and slammed the door—he didn't even say *have a nice day!* —a large delivery truck approached the cab head-on, leaving no room to proceed forward.

Already pissed- off after another miserable start, I banged the cab into reverse and gunned it, barely missing a van pulling into the restaurant's lot. I cranked down my window to cuss out the careless idiot who was *in my way* to discover he was already yelling in my direction. After twenty seconds of colorful back and forth road-raged laced profanity, I realized the puke-green window van looked far too familiar. The other driver again beat me to the punch. "Howie! How are you?"

"Speedy?"

I believe most encounters are by happenstance. However, in every life, a precious few may be predetermined. Call it destiny, for lack of a better word.

Speedy invited me to join him. After a couple minutes of a mutual *how are the wife and kids* exchange, the subject evolved to The Greengrocer. Speedy purchased his business in 1976, eight years prior. To me, it seemed eons ago. He was surprised I was still a cab driver; I guess he expected more from me than I did from myself. We spent a good hour chatting about the store, how he incorporated gourmet food items, exotic cheeses, and even fancy, fresh coffee beans into its offerings. Funny—I always thought coffee grew inside three-pound cans. He talked about the challenges and rewards of running a company but added this: "I'm tired."

I couldn't relate to how owning and running a business could wear a person down yet thought of how stuck and burnt out I felt with my current career path. Speedy then shocked me with another revelation. He was contemplating selling his business and had hoped to run into me. Oddly, during dinner the night before, Chris and I discussed the missed opportunity I had passed by years earlier. I gave Speedy my phone number and said I would talk it over with Chris.

***

It was an idea to explore, for sure. There were a couple of visits, a lunch, some debate. It was clear this would not be a mere job change, but a total commitment. This Greengrocer differed from the place I worked at seven years prior. Despite the regional economic struggles, the neighborhood still thrived. Bus stops on either side of the street produced a healthy volume of walk-up traffic, coupled with a nice array of loyal customers.

Yet, all that glittered was not gold—or even green—in this case. There was a stale vibe, fixtures appeared worn, displays looked half-hearted, and the crew seemed complacent. But I knew those things were fixable. Aside from Speedy's burnout, it became clear The Greengrocer was not as healthy as the name implied. The business was in the red to suppliers, as well as to "Uncle Sam." A recently opened competitor three blocks up-street received positive accolades from the neighborhood while Greengrocer stagnated.

I had more than my share of doubts. I debated it with friends and family. Listed some good old-fashioned pros and cons on notebook paper. Spent sleepless nights tossing and turning, imagining worst- case scenarios and what ifs. Thought about it between and during cab rides. More than a few friends thought it was a bad, even crazy idea, and they made good points. This was the 1980's, the age of the mom-and- pop corner store had come and gone. There were two big Giant Eagle supermarkets on the same street, one only a block away, how could I compete with that? I was still young enough to get a job in my "field"— whatever that had become. The answer became crystal- clear: Yes!

One of the few people who didn't think I was totally nuts was my good friend, Bernie. He encouraged my decision and helped me through the process. We negotiated a price of $12,000 and Bernie helped navigate the financing. For $12K, I obtained a declining business on a great corner, a 1977 aluminum, Ford step-van, the vomit green, rusty Ford Econoline van I almost smashed into, and several rickety display tables. I inherited four of the store's remaining employees—at my will—to assist with the transition, as I did for Speedy years before. Chris, my partner in life, agreed to partner in our new venture.

On June 1, 1984, I turned in my cab for the last time. I misplaced my union withdrawal card long ago but was not going to replace it. I won't be coming back—not anytime soon.

Fred the Cashier wished me good luck. I told him I would weirdly miss the cab, to which he responded, "Don't be a stranger; I'm sure we'll see you again." He then turned to Henry, his cage-mate, once again saying, "They always come back. They just keep coming back."

Howard Johnson's, now a Panera Bread

CHAPTER 19

Greengrocer

1984 - 1996

1974

"Whoa, Nellie! No-oh no, Howie, we never dump our green beans!" Ed spoke in his commanding, yet reassuring tone. "I'm going to make you my protégé. The vegetable stand is a form of art."

Ed launched into a teachable moment, demonstrating his mastery of legume arrangement, forming an upright angled bean blockade in the front area of a shallow rectangular wicker basket, followed by rolling handfuls of string beans into a rippling west to east pattern. After his third methodic rollout, he stepped aside, saying, "Give it a try!"

After my initial thought of 'what the fuck?' I shrugged and attempted to imitate Ed's skillful bean routine. Not as easy as it looked. My beanery did not measure up to the artistry I tried to replicate.

"Not bad, Howie, not too bad," said Ed. "This business, I tell you, I think it's in your blood, you were meant for this."

This statement dumbfounded me, although it would be one of dozens of similar pronouncements by Ed Green. When I started this job, I didn't recognize the difference between a head of cabbage and a head of lettuce, I didn't know a nectarine from a tangerine. I was only the delivery boy who would otherwise sweep, unload watermelons, take out trash, shovel snow, and so forth. There were only a few workers at Ross' Fruit Market, a mom- and- pop corner store, but Ed was the most memorable of the bunch.

Like three other three guys employed at Ross's, Ed was in his late sixties, pushing seventy, semi-retired with decades of produce wisdom and business acumen under his belt. He struck me as someone you would not have messed with in his younger days, sturdily built with thinning close- cropped saltier more than peppery hair and aviator glasses. Ed always sported a lime green blazer, signifying his unofficial doctorate in fruit and vegetable science. The thing that impressed me the most was his extraordinary ability to construct eye-catching, colorful, towering fruit baskets, and wrap, ribbon, and detail them while never removing the cigarette from his mouth or spilling a single ash. One thing I think you, my reader, may conclude from this book; it's hard to phase or impress a seasoned cab driver—a sixteen- year- old—not so much!

***

Ten Years After-

I never came to know how or why Ed Green knew the produce business, *that store,* was inscribed into my DNA. Nevertheless, there I was, a decade later, the sole proprietor of a living, breathing, brick and mortar business.

I thought I started with a slight advantage, having worked there for three years during high school and college, but it wasn't long before reality struck. Sure, I knew the difference between a 56 and an 88- sized Sunkist navel, I could spot the perfect cantaloupe in a pile from 50 feet away, I even remembered the names and idiosyncrasies of many of the loyal customers who still patronized the store. Truthfully, I knew jack-shit. This was an entirely new world; there was much to learn.

My typical day commenced between four and six AM, loading my truck with purchases from various wholesalers spread throughout the produce yards. I had only been there a couple of times in my teenage years, to pick up a case or two of this or that. Fortunately, we inherited a seasoned buyer from Speedy, an older, wiser gentleman named Benny K. Also called brokers, buyers received orders from independent stores, supermarkets, and service wholesalers they represented, procuring merchandise from the various distributors throughout the produce yards. Benny's role was to tailor the product to the unique needs of each client in terms of price, quality, quantity, and other market factors. In the produce industry, green peppers are never just peppers. There are smalls, mediums, larges, extra larges, jumbos, jumbles—yes that is really a produce term—choppers, even suntans. Idaho potatoes, anyone? We have 70s-80s-90s-100s-five or ten pounders, bakers...U.S. #2s will make a fine French fry. Apples? Don't even get me started! This business was more complex than anyone could imagine.

We were the smallest company Benny represented. His fee? How about a whopping seventy bucks per week! For $70, our little store had the same buying power as the big chains and distributors. In a business where commodities can become scarce or double in price overnight due to weather, market conditions, transportation, labor shortages, or a million other things, buying power meant everything!

Benny's "day" usually began around midnight and concluded somewhere between three and five in the morning, depending on his workload. He often finished before I made it to the yards, but my order slips were always ready at a desk in Bachman's Onion House where we often purchased—well, your guess. While he had never visited our store, Benny K remains one of the most influential mentors I ever worked with. He understood our needs and taught me the only thing that mattered was quality. While most stores could get by with the cheap stuff, only the best would do to compete in our area. Benny retired due to health concerns after a couple years, but I will always be grateful.

The yards became an important part of my life over the next eleven plus years. Each morning, I backed my trucks into various loading docks scattered throughout Pittsburgh's famous Strip District. Some of these distributors were housed in an enormous unheated and non- air-conditioned building known as *The Produce Terminal,* which stretched uninterrupted opposite five city blocks. There were also more than a dozen independent distributors on the streets surrounding the gigantic terminal. Every morning required a minimum of two or three hours to inspect and load our merchandise. I learned early on to check everything before it ever touched our trucks. As time went on, I became more hands-on with buying, gaining invaluable insight and experience. On our

busiest days, we picked up from as many as sixteen distributors before heading to the shop.

The Greengrocer was in so many ways the opposite of
the taxi business. While the cab had its steady riders who the
drivers were friendly and familiar with, most taxi rides were
fleeting and temporary encounters, less than a one- night
stand, more like "Hello, how are you, have a nice life."

Owning and running the store, we immersed ourselves
within multiple communities. There were connections with
peers and competitors, alliances with neighboring businesspeople, bonds formed with loyal employees, and special
relationships with our customers. We met some incredible
farmers who delivered top- notch produce to us over the
years, hard- working, fantastic people. With our location
in the heart of Squirrel Hill, we were an integral part of the
neighborhood, embracing the local Jewish community and
our amazing, diverse customer base. Even though my home
is in the suburbs, Squirrel Hill, especially Murray Avenue,
forever remains a part of me.

The yards were another world. Each "house" had its own
unique subculture and personality. For some, rudeness was
simply routine, part of their charm. There was a rough edge;
it was a harsh place to do business. Some of the companies
passed through generations, often from old school Italian
families. Seven years of intensive study at Yellow Cab University made it easier to adapt and integrate into this strange
world. Sales rarely closed with "thank you so much, have
a nice day." It was more like, "Here's your fuckin' pallet of
Broccoli Crowns!" Hey, I could deal with that—even enjoy it.

In the beginning, our biggest obstacle was changing the culture of the store. The Ed Green of yesteryear was gone, along with Greengrocer's once sterling reputation. We took control in June of 1984 with scant working capital and even less knowledge. The lighting sucked, the tile floor was peeling, the walls cried out for fresh paint. The display fixtures were so rickety, one literally collapsed to its death without provocation one afternoon. We inherited a crew who were set in their ways. Green beans were dumped without regard into their allotted cheap plastic display bin. Sorry, Ed.

While I had no idea what I was doing, I knew *something* needed to change. Prior to our first day in business, I met with the employees, offering free reign to use their own ideas and creativity in setting up the store. Upon returning from the yards with my inaugural load, the store remained an exact clone of the way Speedy had left it. So much for that idea.

Meanwhile, my friend Bernie connected us with an accountant to help navigate the financial part of the business. Historically, the store never exceeded north of $200K in gross sales, not a horrific number for a small corner store. When I told the accountant our goal to double that number within four years, he replied it was not a realistic target. I also heard through reliable grapevines that the owner of the shiny, newer market up-street predicted our demise within six months. I was fired up! Motivated. Ready to work!

***

And to work we went. Chris handled much of the paperwork, a monumental task when dealing with multiple vendors daily. We expanded the store hours, opening at six AM, closing at seven PM weekdays, and six on the weekends. We were open most major holidays, usually until mid-afternoon, much appreciated by those last minute, we forgot shoppers. Within three years, we began scheduling employees as early as four AM, setting up the store with meticulous care and detail, replenishing every display. The business prospered and its reputation turned around.

We had two more children, Jenna in '85 and Brian in '87, limiting Chris's role at the store. Our oldest, Justin, was diagnosed with autism at age four. Chris still helped with the bookkeeping and on major holidays, juggling a plateful of responsibility at home. Greengrocer was like raising another child; it had to become *my* baby. My workweeks ranged between 90 and 105 hours, limiting family time, and isolating me from friends. Vacations were rare; the longest one we ever took was three days in San Francisco.

While the business thrived, I often wondered if it was because of me or despite me. We hired some fantastic people who grew with us over the years, while developing a reputation for our fruit and gift baskets. Greengrocer also became a major player in the service wholesale sector, delivering to bars, restaurants, pizza shops, nursing homes, and caterers throughout the region, even landing the concession business at the Pittsburgh Zoo. We became the go-to veggie supplier to the growing community of Asian restaurants—we sold tons of broccoli. The company flourished to the point where our fleet expanded to two box trucks and two full sized delivery vans. We rented a second storeroom across the street to serve as a mini warehouse, transforming it into a fruit basket workshop for the holiday season.

There were major growing pains along the way. The most challenging part of owning any business was playing the role of employer. Within a few months, with one notable exception, the Speedy era crew were gone. Sam, a 75- year- old produce veteran, was a godsend. He shared invaluable business insights. Sam left after about a year when his health declined. We soon added Benny B, an 82- year young fruit merchandiser extraordinaire—no relation to Benny, our buyer. Like Ed, Benny wore his signature green produce doctor's jacket, often complimented with an oversized cowboy hat. Our storefront featured two huge picture windows, piled with tasteful displays of seasonal fruit, complimented by outside sidewalk arrangements of colorful, hardy vegetables. It was commonplace to see photographers or art students taking inspiration from our store's displays, especially Benny's brilliant work. Benny left short of his 86th birthday, passing some months later.

We had so many other great workers, like Nancy, a CMU student with exceptional artistic talent. Nancy designed a new logo, which we had painted on our vans, as well as tee shirts, which we sold in the store. I still have a few even to this day. However, we had our problem employees too.

Like any cash business, employee theft was an issue, even a given. When it got out of hand, we contracted a private detective who would "shop" the employee, document their activity, and eventually confront them in an unexpected, uncomfortable meeting in my office, a concrete dungeon. The interviews always ended with a signed confession and a letter of resignation. We even went a step further and criminally prosecuted four people over the years. This was the part of the business I hated; it made me want out.

While I knew we would not become millionaires, the business was healthy and profitable. We broke that half- million- dollar sales mark in our fourth year and hired a new accountant. Our neighborhood competitor who forecasted our quick demise— he closed his business a couple of years later, becoming our occasional customer and a friendly face.

By 1991, our gross sales exceeded the million- dollar level, something I never imagined would happen. We even landed Poli, the famous seafood establishment three blocks south where so many of my most adventurous cab memories originated. Pittsburgh, being the big- small- town it always was—a good thing—was often behind the times in food trends. Through no genius of my own, Greengrocer was the first to mainstream items like portabella mushrooms, arugula, heirloom tomatoes, and spring mix to the local populace, years before the big stores even knew what they were. We became the go to place for the hard- to- find items. Fresh basil? Always! Pine nuts for your pesto? Sure; Chinese or Portuguese?

Our growth continued, we finally achieved a comfortable income, but the price was steep. Jumping off docks, loading trucks, and stacking coolers took a toll on my back and knees. At thirty-something, I felt old. My kids were growing up fast and I missed out on a lot. The stress level was constant, running a business was a 24/7 job. Although I delegated more authority to our managers, it was always a hands-on affair. I never expected more from my workers than myself, I would not ask them to do something I wouldn't do or hadn't done.

In 1994, we attracted attention from some business brokers, gauging our interest in selling. I was 36; we were at the top of our game, why would I even think about that? So... I began to think about it. Oftentimes, when the 61C bus drove by as we unloaded the trucks, I remarked to whichever helper happened to be there, "You know, that will be me someday." Most of them thought I was nuts, or just an idiot. I was at least halfway serious. When I was growing up, the other kids all wanted to be firefighters, astronauts, center fielders ... my dreams were driving a bus or garbage truck. I was...different.

One of the Asian eateries we serviced opened two locations in the brand- new terminal at Pittsburgh International Airport. The loading docks were located on the same access road as the cabstand. While delivering there, I often observed the airport booming, with taxis moving in and out, weirdly missing my old profession, contemplating if I may someday return.

In late 1994, another stunning surprise came to our family; Chris was pregnant with our fourth. This was a shock, as the medication prescribed for her all but guaranteed having a baby as next to impossible. However, the improbable became reality. I knew I missed the boat with my three older children because of my polygamous marriage to the business and dreaded repeating that process. In January of 1995, during a merciless ice storm, I slipped on ice as I was making my night deposit, landing on my head, rendering me unconscious for at least a minute until an angel motorist stopped and woke me up. The resulting concussion, which I spent two weeks ignoring, transformed my life into a perpetual nightmare for the next six months.

I would frequently forget the topic in the middle of conversations. Life became a giant fog. There were better days and worse ones, but it was a struggle. By late spring, my head began to clear, but my candle was burning out.

Rachel joined our family on June 8, 1995. I know this sounds horrible, but I always thought 99% of all newborns were ugly. She was, really, a beautiful, tiny, five-pound baby. I loved my kids and did not want to miss those milestones and moments again. I called one of those business brokers. It was time.

There was immediate interest. Within a month, we had serious prospects, a father-son team. My accountant thought I was crazy to sell, but my mind was made up. I found a good business lawyer, Kenny, to help seal the deal. After we finished unloading on a muggy July morning, I rushed to our first meeting in an upper- floored office in Oxford Center, a prestigious downtown office tower. Wearing jeans and a sweaty Greengrocer tee shirt, I walked into a roomful of suits. There was my lawyer, the business broker and his assistant, the father and son along with their *two* lawyers and accountant. During the introductions, I learned of junior's recent graduation from a well- regarded university with a shiny new accounting degree; what was I getting into? One of the attorneys handed Kenny and I copies of a "contract" offering a lowball price of $170K, which involved me becoming a savings and loan for a fictitious corporate name. After my laughter subsided, I politely told them to call me back if they decided to be serious. Three days later, the phone rang.

Following two weeks of back and forth, we came to an agreement. For $217,500, they would become the new owners of Greengrocer. They received two trucks and a van, all less than three years old and paid off, all refrigeration equipment and fixtures in the store, and the thing they wanted the most—our good name. There was a long-winded non-compete agreement, listing over fifty wholesale accounts serviced by the store and some weird legalese prohibiting me from selling carrots, parsnips, or rutabagas within x number of miles of the Allegheny or Monongahela Rivers for a y period-of- time. Kenny, my new lawyer friend, advised me to play hardball. I wanted it done; I signed on all the dotted lines.

As part of the deal, I agreed to a hundred- day work contract to help the new ownership's transition. I would work an unprecedented forty- hour workweek for a salary of $700 per week. I was beyond elated at the idea of becoming an employee instead of an employer after all those years!

Eager to be part of the new Greengrocer, I hoped to see the business evolve past the point I was willing to take it myself. In retrospect, this enthusiasm was more selfish than selfless on my part. I wanted The Greengrocer to persevere to preserve my own legacy, so I could tell little Rachel, "That used to be Daddy's store!"

Dave, the new owner, was only twenty-three. He spent time during August working in the store, becoming familiar with the otherworldliness of the yards and meeting the wholesale customers. He wasn't overly gaga with the retail store, which was a concern. I tried to accentuate how retail was the heartbeat of Greengrocer, to little avail, hoping he would come to appreciate the history and community he was about to become part of.

The closing took place in September, with the new owners prepared to take over on the 11th. The transition was a bumpier ride than I had expected. Most of our better employees agreed to stay on, although they were initially upset when I informed them of the sale. I saw Dave as an entitled ex- frat boy but liked and respected his dad. Dave, however, was to be the active partner in the business, with dad there for support.

After a choppy first couple of weeks, things settled down. I had to troubleshoot a couple significant accounts when they felt dissatisfied with product, service, or attitude, but we were able to save them. Dave even asked if I would stay on beyond my contract. I was thrilled, as I didn't exactly have another job waiting in the wings. We had an agreement that my work contract would end on December 21 because our family had a full week's vacation planned. I agreed to return on the New Year and work out amicable employment terms.

The holiday season became stressful. Dave and I were clearly not getting along. I now admit it was partly my stubbornness, wanting to do things my way, but the business was no longer my baby. I decided that I was going to talk to them after my last day and give notice but stay for a short time if they needed me. My phone rang that evening. It was the dad telling me I was fired. Really—they couldn't have done it face to face.

My Greengrocer story reached its end. It was one of the favorite chapters of my life. While my family did not start the business, it became my family business. My dad worked part time in the 1960s for David Ross, the original owner. My brother Ben was the delivery boy for several months, working for Mr. Ross's son, Lou. When Ben took another job, he recommended me to take his spot. I was sixteen, all I wanted to do was drive; how could I say no? Years later, my sister Linda also worked for me for a spell. Of course, my wife went through the heaven and hell of co-owning the place for all those years. There were countless loyal customers and dedicated workers who I'll never forget. Moreover, I had the privilege of working for all four owners, including myself, who sacrificed and committed to being part of a great business legacy. No regrets.

***

Sunday September 10, 1995

My final day as The Greengrocer. Beautiful but bittersweet. We ran down our stock to ease the inventory transition to complete the deal. It was hard to say goodbye to the customers, even more painful to the crew. Even though I would still be there, it was never going to be the same.

Around noon, Tonia, one of our all- time great workers, and I were wheeling some items to our storeroom across the street. As we arrived on the other side, I noticed an elderly lady struggling to parallel park her car. It was the car, a 1980 Chevy Citation in pristine condition, that caught my attention. I decided to assist, guiding her into her space. Smartass that I am, I used exaggerated hand motions as if directing a tractor trailer, while giving Tonia a history lesson about the Citation being advertised with a corny jingle announcing *It's the first Chevy of the 80s.* I have a thing for useless trivia. The lady thanked me for my help as she alighted her vehicle.

"Ma'am, I love your car, want to sell it?" I inquired, eager to diminish my newly found mini- fortune.

"Oh no, I could never do that, this was my husband's last car, I would never sell it." She continued, "I don't think you remember me. We met many years ago."

I was clueless, stuttering, "Um, I-I'm sorry but…"

"That's okay…you're Howie, aren't you?" she said.

I was lost. "Well, uh, yes…I am."

"I'm Mrs. Green, Eddie's wife. He told me last night that you sold your store and I'm so glad I ran into you. Eddie wanted you to know how proud he is of what you did with that place. I promised him I would tell you that."

Tonia looked inquisitive. I was beyond stunned. "Ah, thank you Mrs. Green. Ed was always a great guy; I'll never forget him. Thank you!"

We wished each other the best. Mrs. Green turned and walked slowly down Murray Avenue.

Ed Green? He passed on several years earlier.

Business succeeds because of great employees.
Above: Chris with Tonia;
Below: Howie with Joe "Cheese."

CHAPTER 20

They Always Come Back

January 1996

Freedom! Exiled from my old store, free from the bondage of a business, retired at the ripe old age of thirty-eight. What next?

I could have filed for unemployment, but that was never me. I applied at the local job center for my boyhood dream job of *Bus Operator*, the first of eight such applications I would fill out over the next eighteen months. The word on the street was you had a leg up if you "knew somebody" or were "related." I knew nobody and had few relatives, let alone connected ones. Getting hired at Port Authority based on merit could take a while.

I scanned the help wanted ads for sales positions, hoping for a chance to implement twelve years of retail and account management skills honed from running a company. I was in no hurry, deciding not to jump on anything unless it felt right.

Chris landed a human resources position at a major insurance company, benefiting our family with much needed health coverage. With three 'tween to teens and a baby, I volunteered to transform into Mr. Mom, a stay- at- home dad. This would be temporary, until I found my ultimate job and we felt comfortable placing Rachel in daycare.

I secured an interview for a food service sales position with a well- known, national distributor. The manager who interviewed me was quite familiar with my former business, complimenting me on how difficult it was for his company to crack into any Greengrocer accounts. When he asked about our "secret sauce," perhaps I was too forthcoming when explaining my theory of hard- working chefs' preferences to deal with someone dressed in jeans and a tee-shirt who inspected and loaded their tomatoes at five o'clock that morning in lieu of a nine-to-five salesman with a suit and a price list. He gave me a tour of their new multi- million dollar produce facility, with inventory alphabetized for efficient order fulfillment. He did not seem appreciative when I pointed out how storing avocados with apples—which emit ethylene gas—was never a good idea. The third strike came near the interview's end when I outlined the specifics of the strict noncompete document I signed with my former company. You guessed right. I was not offered the position.

But that was fine, I could play Mr. Mom for a while. I enjoyed being a stay- at- home dad—for a week or two. Within two weeks, I was going nuts being home every day. While Chris had a decent job, it was never going to be enough to feed a family of six, plus two cats. Sure, we had plenty left from the sale of the store, but after our three- day vacation in

Disney, followed by a three- day cruise, topped off with the purchase of a brand- new Toyota Avalon, it was tax time. I always was better at working for money than saving it.

The biggest downfall of Mr. Mom life was my diaper changing methodology. I am a life-long sufferer of the psychological disorder known (by me, at least) as *Poop-a-phobia*, the fear of poop; and/or pee. While the average person simply removes the baby's diaper, wipes her with a wet wipe, maybe two, and replaces the diaper, I had a process! Following the painstaking removal of the soiled diaper, I used a whole new diaper to wipe away any remnants, secured by a third fresh diaper to protect my hands from any possible contact. This was followed by a handful, a cluster of at least a dozen wet wipes to ensure a clean baby's butt before finally putting on diaper number four of the process. I previously used similar routines for my other children, perhaps the reason Chris only resorted to my diaper changing behavior as the nuclear option. Having me as a primary diaper changer was a sure path to bankruptcy.

It became clear that I would never make it as a housespouse. There always was Plan B—perhaps at this point it was Plan C or D? — good old Yellow Cab. I filled out my application to become an *Independent Contract Driver.*

***

The cab company called three days later with an appointment for an interview. The meeting consisted of whether I was still breathing, had a valid license with a clean driving record, and could pass numerous background checks and clearances, along with a multitude of paperwork. I was "hired" a couple of days later and set up for a day of training.

When I sold Greengrocer, I could not wait to make the transformation from employer to employee. The reason I italicized hired was because taxi drivers were no longer company employees; they were independent contractors. Yellow Cab was not technically allowed to fire them either — they could, however, terminate their lease at any time for any reason. So much for job security. While once again a Yellow Cab driver, I was essentially self- employed. When I departed in 1984, I was one of a handful of remaining unionized drivers. By the end of that year, the company had gone 100% lease.

Training day felt more like a reorientation. They explained the leasing system, the different options available (10 hours, 24 hours, weekends) and the general workings of the system. We took a ride to the airport, where we met the curb superintendent, a county employee overseeing all forms of ground transportation. This airport was so much larger and had twice as many rules as the old terminal. Upon our return to Yellow Cab's offices, I ran into one of the radio dispatchers from the good old days. He asked how my dad was doing and his next question was one which I would hear for years, sometimes to this day: "What happened?"

People who have never owned and operated a business could never understand how one may simply choose to sell, or even walk away. They assume the worst. Did the business fail, did you screw up, burn out, succumb to drug addiction, go bankrupt? It is hard for someone to comprehend that it may have been time to make a change. I told him the truth; I sensed he believed me, but if not…oh well.

Unlike the "good old days," there was now only one garage, the same Centre Avenue Garage in East Liberty where I spent my previous years with Yellow. They still owned the Manchester facility, but it was used exclusively for their school and shuttle van business. The Checker model taxis, the only ones I ever drove, were ancient history. The fleet now consisted of reconditioned Ford Crown Victoria's and Chevy Caprices and Impalas, many being former police cars. Under leasing, the gas now came out of our own pockets and these cars were not exactly fuel efficient. The cost of doing business—I already knew too well.

The day ended with us having our pictures taken and being branded with a new driver's number. I asked if I could have my old one, #505, but was told those three- digit numbers were commission only and retired years ago. My new name would be Driver# 9694. I was given a new I.D. to display in the taxi, a laminated yellow card with my mug and my newest identity, 9694, in bold black print, and told I could start as soon as the next day.

The following afternoon, I reported for the first day of act two of my cab career. It was rather strange, walking into the same garage as I had hundreds of times before, yet feeling "new." As I approached the cage, I was immediately comforted by the sight of two familiar figures working the windows. As much as most things constantly change, others never do.

"Holy crap, Fred —you're right again!" Henry proclaimed to his work partner. "They really all do come back."

Fred glanced away from the transaction he was processing, chuckled, and shook his head, his professorial eyewear angling halfway down his nose. "I told you a million times, Henry; they always come back…they just keep coming back."

"Oh my god, its Little Max!" A voice shouted from another part of the garage. I turned and waved at a familiar face—*but what was his name?*

At that moment, I realized I was back.

The Checkers are now ancient history.

CHAPTER 21

Transitions

1996-1997

"I told you a million times, Henry, they always come back... they just keep coming back," Fred declared to his cage partner and everyone within earshot.

Henry chuckled as he slid a blank trip sheet and set of keys through the windows' open slot. "Welcome home, Howie—take cab 400—he's off tonight."

"Thanks; good to be back again." I headed for the lot and found my evening work companion, a beat-up Chevy Impala with *only* 378,000 miles of experience. The good-old Checkers from "back in my day" were ancient, though cherished history. The mileage logged in those cabs was always a mystery, as their odometers offered only five digits, zeroing out each 100,000 miles.

Other than yellow paint with black and white checkered trimming, everything about the fleet was different. A divergent blend of refurbished police and rental cars—full-sized

Chevys, Fords, even several minivans, supplanted the out-moded Checkers. Updated, lighter equipment replaced the oversized, trunk- mounted tubular radios and bulky steel meters of yesteryear. There were even some luxury cars, several new Cadillacs, and Oldsmobile Ninety-Eights, on loan from General Motors as test cars. GM and Yellow Cab made a deal, with the caveat of limiting each car to regular drivers and keeping them clean, while allowing data collection, maintenance, and monitoring by GM engineers and technicians. It was a good deal for GM, Yellow Cab, the assigned drivers, and pleasantly surprised passengers.

As much as the songs felt so different, so many lyrics remained the same. My first trip of the 1990's, as luck would have it, asked, "how long have you been driving a cab?" I should have been prepared with a snappy answer to that universal conversation starter. Instead, I tortured my poor passengers, a lovely older couple, with a word and number salad including seven years, eighteen years, and twenty minutes—all in a single sentence. I was even confused after that. Yes, I had seven years of experience which began eighteen years earlier but had only been back for twenty minutes after an eleven year "coffee break." By the end of their fifteen- minute trip, I think they sort of understood my complicated answer to their simple question.

Soon enough, I realized despite my prolonged leave of absence, I still qualified for the cabbies' monopoly on single syllable nicknames. On any random evening, I could be *Boss, Bub, Bud, Chief, Guy, Man, Pal*—or on rare occasions, a version of *Sir,* with varying undertones ranging from condescending to respectful. As comfortable as I was with being a bub, or even a chief for short intervals, it was time to embrace more current temporary identities—like *Bro, Dude,* or *Skip.* Those took time and effort to adjust to; especially, Dude!

I noticed the changing demographics among my fellow drivers. Some of the "old-timers" were long gone, yet many endured, entrenched within an ever- evolving cab culture. There was a notable percentage of all-in, 24- hour, seven- day leasers, although a smaller share of the *this is my other job* crowd remained. Due to insurance regulations, the mini-mum age to lease a taxi increased from 18 to 25. This was more related to Yellow's transformation into a glorified car rental company than any conscientious effort to build a co-hesive, mature workforce.

It was a shame that an opportunity afforded to me at such a young age to finance my education was no longer an option for subsequent generations. When I began cabbing as a student, I often crossed paths with peers who also taxied their way through academia. As valuable as formal higher education was, few jobs provided more comprehensive life experience than this one. Yellow Cab University, in innumer-able ways, shaped the person I became.

We part-timers often waited an hour or more at the garage until cabs became available. Leaning against and sit-ting on the hoods of parked cabs awaiting repair, we often compared notes. There were the inevitable Pitt students who hung around for a summer, even some high school teachers. I was impressed by one guy I met at the airport completing his law degree, financed by three years of hardcore driving. One of the most prominent ex-cabbies I encountered, Rich Fitz-gerald, cabbed his way through Carnegie-Mellon, eventually serving several terms as Allegheny County Executive—one of the top elected positions in our state's political landscape. And speaking of accomplished Yellow Cab alumni, Frances Arnold began driving right after high school, being one of the youngest and few female drivers in the mid-1970s. Dr. Arnold would eventually be awarded The National Medal of Technology from President Barack Obama, a Nobel Peace Prize in Chemistry, and later be named a key member of President Biden's Science Team. Not a bad trip for an ex- cab driver!

Among the current pool of drivers, a notable difference was an uptick in diversity. During its Checker days, most of Yellow Cab's drivers were white and male, with perhaps fifteen to twenty percent comprising of black males. Females and immigrants each could be counted on either hand.

White men now accounted for a bare majority. There were noticeably more African Americans, along with a significant influx of foreign- born drivers, an eclectic mix of Asian, African, Eastern European, and Middle Eastern descendants. Female drivers, seldom seen in my earlier years of cabbing, were now more commonplace—a welcome and overdue evolvement of a cab company at least starting to reflect the world who patronized it.

While joining a heterogeneous workforce was a positive, there were inevitable side effects. Although racism thrived in the 1980s, I only recalled sporadic instances of passengers expressing gratitude for being chauffeured by a white guy. After a few weeks back on the job, it was hard not to notice my whiteness being a conversational icebreaker for some riders. At times I couldn't tell if they were commenting or complimenting, whether it was an anomaly or an achievement.

Occasionally, I double checked my hand or arm color to confirm this implied privilege. Even more often, people expressed varying forms of surprise or appreciation for getting an "American" cab driver, or one who spoke English. While I wasn't exactly the grammar police, it was hard to hold my tongue when those praising my native dialect could barely construct a sentence. Sometimes I offered a snide or subtle retort, but usually shut up and went with their program, hoping to salvage a decent tip.

It took time to get reacclimated, particularly adapting to the mindset of being an independent operator rather than an employee. While the essence of the profession—seeking out people willing to pay for rides between points A and B—remained intact, the culture evolved to more of a business, and less of the hustle I recalled. Eleven- plus years at the helm of a challenging business helped ease this adjustment.

A sizable portion of our evening business included folks working overtime at their respective downtown offices, mostly corporate, accounting, and law firms. They often rode public transit or carpooled to work while being rewarded with cab fare home, usually paid in the form of company vouchers. When dispatched for these trips, even though there were only one or two cab orders heard over the radio, I often observed multiple taxis lurking in front of the buildings upon my arrival. Most of these cabs shared a single commonality—an extra antenna attached to the roof.

I soon learned these drivers were members of *groups*—also referred to as *systems*. The groups were prime examples of the transition of taxi driving from a hustle to a more enterprising venture. While cabbies always had steady riders, they now often worked together, in co-op arrangements covering their own and their peers' regular trips. Several groups existed, some involving only two or three drivers, others numbering over twenty. Each had "leaders" who managed the group phone—cellphones of the 1990s were awkward, bulky, and usually lugged around in vinyl bags or small boxes. The system drivers paid weekly fees for access to auxiliary two- way radios, plugging the units into the cigarette lighters inside their cabs. These groups functioned like mini franchises within the cab company, and though they siphoned business away, Yellow Cab loved it. More riders calling their personal drivers decreased the need for in-house operators and dispatchers, enabling payroll reductions in those departments.

Several drivers from the more prominent groups invited me into their ranks. At first, I was skeptical, hearing the pros and cons from both groupies and fellow solo flying independents. The thought of shelling out weekly dues and abandoning the random unpredictability I loved about cab life sowed doubt. After a week or two of internal back and forth, I decided to try it out. It was evident that the groups had a healthy chunk of the company's more desirable trips and regulars tied up.

I enlisted with one run by Mike and Carl, two veteran drivers. Their group boasted a solid client base, including several prestigious law firms. For my $25 weekly donation, I was gifted an extra radio, a packet of business cards, and the designation of *Unit 6*. The group trips were a decent supplement rather than a substitute for my normal driving routine. From day one, I embraced a rainmaking role, recruiting new riders; carding workers—secretaries, lawyers, servers, shift workers, along with a few regular bargoers who tipped well. Two of my favorite steadies included a married couple of bingo players who rode from their Tuesday evening downtown game to Spring Hill, a mini mountain neighborhood to the north. Jim and Betty raised ten children and I forget how many grandkids and were always great company for their quick ride across the Allegheny. I began treating my job as a business. Sure, I hustled and played salesman, bringing added revenue to our group, yet there was a renewed comfort level—the businessperson I had been for the past dozen years never left. And business was always as much about fostering relationships as earning a profit. That saying—it's just business, nothing personal—was so untrue. Successful business *is* personal.

While readapting well to cab-life, I had no steady cab. My cage confined buddies tried to hook me up with something decent most days but there were no guarantees. Although the GM luxury test cars were restricted, I was deemed the backup driver on Cab 198, an appropriately numbered Oldsmobile Ninety- Eight. The regular driver, a kindly man with a good ninety years of life under his belt, nicknamed *Father Time*, decided to cut back, transitioning into *Father Part Time*. Within a month, I was awarded custody of 198, with Father Time content to drive on my days off. It was a boat of a cab, with a luxurious leather interior, a superb sound system, and other bells and whistles one expects in a carmaker's flagship model. Having a work partner of such magnitude helped boost my quest for new group business, and surely did not hurt the tips.

***

It was nice to be back. Our city, my big-small town, was now a thriving place, part of a robust new economy. The Promised Land, with its new terminal, was busier than ever, fulfilling the nickname. I lucked into having one of the premier cars in the fleet to drive every day. With a growing roster of regular riders, I was assured of them being treated well by my group partners when I was unavailable. Many of the system trips paid extremely well, with the camaraderie among my fellow groupies a bonus. Between Yellow Cab radio, our group, and increased tourism in a revived city, I was in a good place, making excellent money.

As well as things were going, my post-Greengrocer aspiration of transitioning from an employer to an employee endured. Yes, I was thrilled to rejoin the cab world, but realized I remained self- employed, restricted to Yellow Cab's non-negotiable discretion and terms. It was a comfortable living with uncomfortable job security. My eyes and ears were open for better opportunities, while always on the ultimate prize: Port Authority bus operator—a union job with great benefits.

After filling out multiple applications and passing the written test the *second* time—I swear I answered each question the same the first time—a letter of acceptance arrived. My newest career would begin on December 1, 1997. Bus operators were reputed to be well compensated, with the caveat of a three year pay progression to top rate. At 65% of the full hourly rate, this meant an initial drastic income reduction. The long- term outlook outweighed the pay cut. And I promised my old crew at the store I would one day drive the bus. I even picked up a couple of them by chance, which was more than cool—that big, small-town thing again.

The transition to a bus operator felt natural, still transporting the public, albeit on a magnified scale. And anyone who patronizes public transit can attest to the never-ending and interesting drama occurring aboard forty- foot long, heavily populated vehicles. My Yellow Cab educational advantage eased the culture shock of life in the driver's seat of a bus—it takes a lot to phase a seasoned cabby. And while enthralled with my new career, I was always a cab driver at heart. Supplementing my temporarily reduced income by making the cab my "this is my second job-job" was an easy call.

Driving only a few days per month brought inevitable changes. It was no longer viable financially to stay with the group and I had to kiss my baby, 198 cab, goodbye. I would miss driving Sharon home to East McKeesport after her twelve- hour days at the law office, Sandy from US Steel Building to Murrysville, Kathleen riding to her night shift from Larimer to a North Side packaging factory—but I knew they would all be in good hands with my old group buddies.

Secure full- time employment, with paid vacations, sick days, and holidays; health, dental, and eye care; and especially, a pension to look forward to, was the perfect prescription for this forty- year- old father of four kids and two cats. For the first time in thirteen years, I was an actual employee, and thrilled with it. Taxi driving would become my side hustle again, for the first time since college, and I was fine with that. I would work when I wanted, when I could, or when I needed, starting when I wanted and stopping after I had enough. After each week on the bus, as interesting as the eclectic mix of passengers could be, I looked forward to not knowing who to expect or where I would go. There were airport trips. Railroad crews. Drunks. Partiers. Strippers. Workers. Students. Tourists. Steeler fans. Convention goers. And yes—even drug runs.

Meter's running.

Examples of some of the buses and routes which I was often assigned from Port Authority's Harmar Garage.

CHAPTER 22

Pharmaceutical Sales

April 1997

Nothing sounded atypical about the radio call I snagged in Dormont, a nearby middle- class community, on a cool, drizzly Wednesday evening. I slowed the taxi to a halt, noticing two young men, mid- twenties at a stretch, emerging from an ordinary brick dwelling. Probably on their way to a South Side watering hole— nothing extraordinary here.

Both rear doors opened and closed in unison. "Hey guys, where we headed?"

They glanced at each other, momentarily hesitating. "Um," the one on the right spoke first, "how about, like, Mercy Hospital?"

My seventh sense, *cabby sensory perception,* kicked into gear. It was just after eight, an odd time for a shift change. Neither wore scrubs or any semblance of hospital attire. I observed no profuse bleeding, no apparent signs of physical distress. Visiting hours would be winding down. *Oh yeah, one of these…* I decided to play along for the time being.

"Do you want to be dropped off at the main entrance, the annex, the parking garage, or the E.R.?" I quizzed, already aware of the upcoming answer—None of the above.

As we hung a left onto West Liberty Avenue towards downtown, the other guy clarified,. "We're actually going up by Mercy, like, near Fifth Avenue."

The red flags now flew at full staff. "And this would be your… final destination?" I asked, prepared for the predictable reply.

They looked at each other again, then back at me. "So, we'll only be, like, two minutes, tops. Could you wait and bring us back to Dormont?"

Ah, yes…the good, old round trip. Been there, done that. "Sure. Forty bucks. Upfront."

The man in the passenger side looked at his buddy, somewhat puzzled. He knew as well as I did that the round trip, including their brief stop, would run maybe $20, certainly less than $25 on the meter. He also realized I knew exactly what they were up to, as he reached into his pocket, peeling off two twenties from a wad of folded money and passed them over the seat, saying, "we appreciate you."

As we sped through The Liberty Tubes, it was time to inform them of the ground rules.

"Nobody else gets into this cab, no one even approaches the cab, nothing gets passed through your windows, this ain't a mobile drive thru…"

The man seated behind me interjected, "Hey dude, we do this all the time in taxis. We just gave you forty dollars!"

"Sorry, not in this one." I continued, "I'm fine with dropping you off in the hood, you can find another cab and just pay me the fare…"

"No, it's cool, we want you to stay," said the other partner-in-crime.

"Okay, then," I took charge again, "this is how we roll. We'll pull over about a half block before the gas station. You guys get out, go down the street, do your thing, which I have no idea what that may be, and come back. You have five minutes max, and I'm gone— with or without you."

They found these terms amenable. The lone neighborhood gas station was more of a point of reference than a center for commerce, illuminating the nearby storefronts, side streets, and alleys where multiple pharmaceutical sales representatives often congregated. I scoped out an easily escapable parking spot up-street and they alighted the taxi. I watched them duck into a darkened doorway several houses down, and within two minutes, we were on our way.

With mission accomplished, they opted to be dropped off at a local bar in Beechview, closer to town than the original pick up, to share their acquired good fortune with some friends. They were pleased with the service, as the guy who complained earlier handed me an extra fin.

Forty-five bucks for some twenty minutes of work; good deal! They got their goodies. The pharmaceutical distribution industry got their cut— not a bad trip.

CHAPTER 23

Tunnel of Love

May 1998

T*his* never gets old...

Not even after doing it thousands upon thousands of times. At any and every imaginable hour. Day. Night. Dusk. Dawn. Especially at night. In. Out. In and out. Preferably with company, an accomplice, a willing partner. Most satisfying with a virgin. All the better with a group! I often fly solo, but still find it gratifying. The entire process lasts but a minute, a little longer if I slow the pace; its climax bursts into euphoric specters of shapely, towering erections sprouting from vibrant landscapes. And *this* only ever occurs within a singular place on the entire planet.

This, of course, refers to the city-bound ride through our Fort Pitt Tunnels and over our Fort Pitt Bridge. No place else, no city on Earth, has an entrance rivaling the 'Burgh's. Only here can you transcend a steep-graded highway enveloped by lush greenery and plow through a mile- long illuminated hole inside a mountain to be greeted with an explosive kaleido-scope of stunning architecture eclipsed by an array of bridges crossing a trio of merging resplendent rivers.

If you've never known this pleasure, tune in to any na-tionally televised Steeler's home game or Pittsburgh-centric documentary. The media seldom resist the temptation of zooming through a vehicle's windshield as it spills from the mighty tunnel's mouth to witness the city's proud proclama-tion: *This* is us!"

One of the finest perks of cabbing is playing the role of ambassador for my hometown. When ferrying virgin visitors from the airport, I have no standard playbook for their inau-gural entrance. At times, I prepare them, encouraging them to have eyes wide open as the tunnel's end comes into view. On rare occasions, I'll do a countdown. When escorting Steeler fans for their first pilgrimage, I ensure they focus left, where the Allegheny surrenders to the Ohio River, as Heinz Field for them is a shrine. But most of the time, I say nothing, offer no preamble as the breathtaking view holds its own, speaks for itself.

Despite this visual orgasm, those few seconds crossing the bridge—at 750 feet, a short span—can be a daunting task. Two fast moving lanes of post-tunnel traffic merge with a heavily traveled on-ramp from the left into an instant four-lane cluster of crisscrossing motorists, guided by a confusing assortment of overhead directional signs pointing towards three major off ramps, each with their own multiple offshoots on the downtown side of the bridge. Yet, nothing about this nightmarish traffic pattern can ever diminish the view.

As exhilarating as our city's entrance is, the reverse ride is anticlimactic at best. Sure, a glance from the back or side window of the taxi as it ascends the bridge's lower deck may offer one final glimpse of inclines scaling Mt. Washington, or a fond farewell to our North Shore. Within seconds, the tunnel swallows us, leaving it all behind. Nothing exciting greets us at the outer end unless the tunnel crew's maintenance facilities and service trucks float your boat. Ahead, an uphill ribbon of monotonous concrete congestion awaits, along with a side view of trees and the endless suburban sprawl typifying every metropolis, U.S.A. The outbound ride away from the city through the tunnels is as unremarkable as the inbound ride is invigorating. And I've driven it so many thousands of times over the years, and it's always the same. Bland. Ordinary. Boring. Every time—except for just once. Only this one time.

"Has anyone ever had sex in your cab?" forever remains among the top five most peppered questions at cabbies from all-too curious passengers.

Unless I am in a jovial mood or have an acute sense of an elaborate response yielding a significant uptick of financial reward my way upon reaching our destination, my usual answer is an annoyed grunt, or "yeah, sure," or a sarcastic "all the time."

The truth? It depends upon one's definition of "sex in a cab." It wouldn't be far-fetched to assume a few of my customers have engaged in some other version of a ride while I was giving them one. I may have been too busy doing my job, as in *driving*, to focus on the activities in the back seat. I recall too many late- night post bar scene trips transporting couples, people "hooking up" (I used to associate that word coupling with the towing industry— who knew?) engaged in obvious foreplay, but all-in, committed intercourse? A hard one to answer. There was one trip in the Checker days of the 1980s while navigating through a torrential thunderstorm after a pick-up at The House of Tilden, a popular gay after-hours spot, there were grounds for reasonable suspicion of a blow- job in progress behind my head. But I can't verify that, as I was far more concerned with the hazardous road conditions than any ongoing oral escapades. And I chose not to further investigate, throwing the garage's gas attendant an extra dollar to park the taxi, leaving any forensic evidence for another to discover. I do remember those passengers tipping very well after the trip—perhaps they simply appreciated my professional driving.

Yet, the most persistent curiosity seekers refuse to accept my nonchalance or maybe, maybe not, as an answer. "So, seriously, has anyone ever actually done it in your cab or not?"

Okay, all right, I give up! Yes. Only this one time. The lone single incident which I unequivocally documented full throttle taxicab copulation, an absolute ride within the ride.

I banged a radio call from The Decade, an iconic Pittsburgh rock and roll go-to, where the likes of Cindy Lauper, Bon Jovi, and Springsteen were reputed to cameo. My usual expectation at this place was to park the cab, see the bouncer, and wait for my fare to finish their drink, pay their tab, or scoop their friend from the bathroom floor. This time, a man and a woman in their thirties were ready to rock, his hand meeting my passenger door's handle as I pulled up.

"Do you know the Viking Motel, on Banksville Road?" the man asked.

"Sure thing," came my reply. Good deal. A quickie! A five-mile ride to the first exit outside the tunnels. Easy money.

The woman had a round, pretty face with deep-set ocean blue eyes, and long, straight blackish hair, styled in the formation of a classic rock loving mullet. Tall, attractive, and slightly big boned, she wore a short jean skirt flanked by a light-colored, lower cut top, revealing boobs of significance. She had a newfound friend, the drummer of the hair band who landed that evening's gig. Ah, the rock and roll life! You go guy!

While I had my work ear on the radio, strategizing the next trip, my eavesdrop ear overheard the woman confide about her break- up six months earlier and how long it had been since she last got laid. It quieted down a bit, and within a minute, the familiar sounds of wet lip-smacking replaced any verbiage. I figured the part of Banksville Road in front of their motel destination could soon assume the temporary nickname of *Bangsville Road*. My companion for the evening was a retired Chevy Caprice police cruiser— those cars could fly! As we merged onto a near empty highway, I nailed the gas pedal with a heavy foot, loving the sound of the powerful engine finding life. A momentary glance in the rear- view mirror revealed the Chevy not to be the only thing in vigorous motion.

The woman aggressively unbuckled her rock star's belt, as he slumped into the confines of the cab's bountiful back seat. Within seconds, her top draped the seat's left side headrest; she was moving, taking full charge. I'm just driving the car, trying to tell myself this is all strictly routine. As we merged onto the deck of the Fort Pitt Bridge, the top of his head sunk below the top of the seat, his newfound friend on top, skirt hiked up, riding like she was determined to win the sex rodeo.

Amidst a mix of enthusiastic *ooohs aaahs, yesses* and *ohs,* we penetrated the tunnel's left lane, passing numerous cars, most of the drivers doing a double take. I could see the man in the car behind me enough to notice a "what the..." look on his face. This couple were without a doubt engaged in a full- throttled tunnel-fuck!

They dismounted as we hit the Banksville exit, seemingly elated with their encounter. I didn't know whether to laugh, cry, or ask "how was everything?" As we pulled into the Viking's lot, the woman apologized, something to the effect of, 'I couldn't wait, it had been so long,' while her companion shrugged and tipped a twenty.

You want details? I don't know; I'm not a porn writer—the guy didn't even have a porn moustache! I can't say for sure if there were any pulsating rods, quivering thighs, molten hot flesh; sorry, I did not even want to pay *that* close attention. But the one memory I have is this: All I could think about as we sped away from those tunnels was, "What was the guy behind us thinking as he witnessed this love tunnel extravaganza?"

CHAPTER 24

Promised Land

2000

I t would be remiss to pen a memoir of taxi life and exclude this word: Airport. It would be unimaginable to exit the ground transportation doors at any major terminal without spotting parades of taxis picking up, dropping off, or waiting in never-ending queues.

In Pittsburgh, each cabby has some degree of a relationship with the airport. Some harbor an anti-relationship, wanting absolutely nothing to do with the place. Even if they land a trip there, for them, there is no promise, choosing not to even entertain the idea of sitting in the line of awaiting taxis for that luck-of-the-draw fare. They may have been psychologically scarred of the memory of a four hour wait, only to be rewarded with a $10 trip to the edge of the airport property. These things happen all the time. Or they do not wish to participate in, or even casually observe the social—and often anti-social—banter among angry, bored, or frustrated airport lot junkies.

I place myself in the category of drivers I refer to as "frequent- flyers." We love our airport trips, but do not live or die by the airport's unspoken promises. We know how to "play cab driver" without it. My strategy is to find *one out* –an airport trip—from the city or a distant suburb, then line up, hoping to *get a good one* on the return. The logic of getting one out, followed up with one in, is to build a nice base, a cushion towards one's daily expenses while burning minimal miles and fuel. Sometimes that airport trip is nowhere to be found. On those days, I become cab driver, careening throughout the county, pin-balling from one trip to the next. As a frequent flyer, I will often take a shot at The Promised Land, shifting later in the evening, especially if a major event or convention is coming to town.

And for our final category, we have the regulars, the diehards. These are the lifers, who cannot resist the lure, the hope of a long one, biding the bulk of their waking and many of their sleeping hours in the holding lot, awaiting their destiny—or at least a destination. The airport is all they know, who they are. No matter where their trip goes, they are pre-programmed to switch into automatic pilot, directly back to the 'port. They are entrenched in this ritual, addicted to whatever unfulfilled promises are in store.

An enormous concrete parking area, the holding lot is the staging area shared by taxis, limousines, parking shuttles, and chartered buses. It is divided into five lanes, with the three on the left reserved for the taxicab lines. To enter, all vehicles have a sensor in the windshield to magically raise the metal gate arm. Upon arrival, we choose one of the lanes, writing down the last cab in each to track when it becomes our turn to proceed to the terminal. Astute drivers take the precaution of jotting down at least three or four numbers from each lane, in case someone leaves, or idiotically decides to switch lines. The unwritten rule is to commit to one lane. When full, the lot accommodates a good eighty taxis.

A hodge-podge of other ground transportation professionals occupies the remainder of the lot. There is not much socializing between the cabbies and the others. When limos and black cars gained increased prevalence at the airport in the early 1990s, the die-hards bitched and moaned about the limos "stealing our business." As time evolved, the presence of large numbers of limos evolved into a welcome sight, signaling the arrivals of substantial flights, translating into a healthy volume of cab business. My personal take has always been that limo drivers are simply cab drivers wearing bad suits.

A small concrete building abuts the left side of the holding lot, housing a well-worn picnic bench, vending machines, and two gender designated bathrooms. The vending machines offer such delicacies as overpriced chips cusping upon their expiration dates, as well as a hot, disgusting, sludgy substance dispensed in too-thin cups masquerading as coffee. Having never ventured into the ladies' restroom, I can only testify to the repulsiveness of the men's facilities. A long-past its lifespan, formerly stainless- steel sink under an adjoining germ-festive hand dryer which seldom functions, shares the right wall with two rusted out metal urinals. These are undoubtably the original installed fixtures from when the airport's new terminal opened in 1992; far too much pee to imagine! In the rear of these luxurious quarters is one lone toilet stall, which I proudly proclaim to have never set foot within. I have reached the point where no matter how long the wait, I will never again partake in the coffee/sewage machine. The last time I did, I was treated to the bonus of a dead fly floating in my cup. If a long wait looks to be in order—these days, it is a given—I utilize the safer restrooms at the Hyatt Regency on airport property, or stroll down to the terminal, where decent coffee can also be had.

The wait is an experience in and of itself. Everyone has their routines. Many, including myself, often insulate themselves in the limited world that is their cab. They read, worship their electronic gods, they think, reflecting on what could have been if only this or that, or fondly remember what once was. The few who have not completely given up hope dream of what could be. The health-conscious choose moderate exercise, pacing up and down the endless rows of cabs. Small groups inevitably form, with drivers comparing notes and socializing, often evolving into bitch-fests about rude people, the lameness of the company, politics, Uber hatred, or whatever the issue du-jour happens to be. Some of the Muslim faithful proceed to the grassy areas surrounding the yellow ocean of cabs, prayer rugs in tow. They pray facing east, in the direction of Mecca, or Pittsburgh's

East End. Surely their prayers come from the heart, but I sometimes wonder whether they are asking Allah for world peace, or a $300 trip.

And more than a few drivers congregate into one of the van cabs for a friendly game of cards, sometimes shortly after offering their prayers. If there is an occupation on the planet compatible with gambling, this would be the one.

The wait time can range anywhere from zero to four or five hours. When a cab driver happens upon an empty lot, the Promised Land fulfills its promise as he scoots to the terminal to find a line of awaiting customers. Once a frequent occurrence, this is now seldom seen. The typical wait averages around two hours. Long, but bearable.

During slow holiday weeks, the waiting can be excruciating as the holiday approaches. Many drivers simply leave after dropping off, but diehards and some frequent flyers wait it out, no matter what. Here it is again—that cab driver's high risk gambling instinct kicking into overdrive. Most of the year, the bulk of trips go towards Downtown or Oakland, the business, education, and medical hearts of the city. On holidays, most trips go anywhere else. There are more than a decent percentage of fares to distant towns and bordering states, making those long waits worth the gamble. But every lucky coin has its flip- side, often turning that forever wait into short runs to nearby communities like Clinton, Coraopolis, Imperial, or Robinson Township. For me, this is the beauty of the job. On any given night, one may be rewarded with a short and disappointing trip to the closest exits off the parkway, only to return to an empty lot, and waiting loads at the terminal's taxi stand. As he loads the passenger's luggage and hears "Latrobe"—a $180 trip—the thankful cabby looks up, paying a silent tribute to the Airport gods, as The Promised Land finally lives up to its name.

The holding lot at The Promised Land.

Airport taxi stand.

Getting to The Promised Land was half the battle.

CHAPTER 25

Workaholism

2001

My career—aka "real job" was going well. The plan was to remain in the bus seat for three or four years before exploring other opportunities within Port Authority, such as the routing and scheduling department, or supervision.

After only a year and a half of living out my childhood bus driving fantasy, the novelty began to wear off. I loved the work, but in June 1999, an opportunity with a hefty pay bump presented itself. I applied for, and was offered, the supervisory position of dispatcher. It was not my dream job, but with my kids approaching college age, it was a sensible shoe to try on.

A public transit dispatcher is a more multi-dimensional position than radio dispatching for Yellow Cab, or AAA. While having access to and monitoring the bus radio channels, we rarely engaged—a good thing. The road supervision was handled by *traffic,* the Authority's jargon for bus radio communicators. As division dispatchers, we occupied caged offices not unlike the ones where Freddy, Henry, and the other cashiers encamped inside the taxi garages. Our primary responsibility involved logistics, as in overseeing that the contractually correct asses occupied the drivers' seats of the scheduled buses at their designated times and places.

I would spend the next twenty-two years in that department, working shifts in all five bus divisions, as well as sporadic overtime guest appearances at South Hills Village Rail Center, which I dubbed *The Little Railroad and Village*. The job is a demanding one, where we serve as liaisons between the company and drivers' union—an acrobatic balancing act, as we all belong to that same local. In addition to maintaining thousands of hours of minute-by-minute service, we needed to be experts on and enforcers of the driver's union contract, payroll, work assignments and every other unforeseeable issue which arose..

Cab driving became a nice escape valve from that grind. After all these years, I continued to embrace the randomness, and yes, the risks, that came with each trip in those distinctive yellow cars. Even so, it was difficult to hit the cab gig with any consistency. At the Authority, we picked our scheduled shifts based upon departmental seniority, where I was far down on the list. My turns involved working *knockouts*—combinations of mixed early, middle, and midnight shifts. Even with consecutive days off, it was often less than a 48-hour break, allowing time for only one taxi lease.

When I could squeeze in time for Yellow Cab, I sometimes had to wait for hours to secure a decent vehicle. There were more drivers than ever, with never enough equipment to go around. At the bus company, they paid drivers for their time when there were not enough buses to fulfill the schedule, which happened with unacceptable frequency. Cabbies, on the other hand, were forced to linger around the garage, awaiting the opportunity to pay the company for the privilege of renting a car. I appreciated that the Yellow Cab cage dwellers tried their best to find me a good cab—there were plenty of bad ones—but I became less patient than in my younger years, in the previous century.

Nevertheless, it was great money for a part- time gig, comparable to my base pay at job number one, and the immediate reward of cold cash was always gratifying. However, premium paid overtime was available at Port Authority, which I accepted often, allocating even less time for the cab. Yellow Cab's *if you show up at least once a month* standard remained in effect but was enforced with more vigor. By 2001, I was barely meeting that stipulation but was fine with only keeping my foot in the door while the cab company likely couldn't have cared less.

As a dispatcher, I was able to pick a summer vacation week, something that takes a decade's worth of seniority to even sniff as a bus operator. Not about to let that go to waste, we used it for a family trip to Ocean City. Coupled with the overtime I scored at job one, there was little time for my side job. Through spring and summer, I worked just a few shifts at Yellow, although some were the sixty-hour, weekend leases. The last time I worked that summer was a weekender at the beginning of August.

August was hectic at the Authority, but I managed to squeeze in some vacation days for a weekend getaway. I planned on cabbing at least part of Labor Day weekend to stay in the game, but a double overtime shift squashed that. Still, I wasn't worried; the cab people would let me slide for a week or two. Afterall, I had been there forever.

Then, it happened. September 11th.

It was my day off. I was lounging in bed at nine-something when my wife rushed in and told me I needed to turn on the TV. Minutes later, the phone rang. It was Danny, my cohort from West Mifflin Division. "We could use help, can you get here, ASAP?" Of course…

Like most Americans, I was shocked. Devastated. Would our lives ever be the same? The furthest thing from my mind was driving any cabs anywhere.

After a few more weeks, now October something, I realized it was way past time to make one of my Yellow Cab cameo appearances. There seemed to be more taxis parked in the yard than usual; my gut said a lot of drivers were staying home. My old buddy, Henry, was working in the cage. "Howie; haven't seen you for a while. Let's find you a good one. Hey—they have you flagged in the system," Henry continued, "Just go upstairs. I'll call and tell them you're good to go; they'll give you a return slip."

"Sure, thanks Henry, I'll go up," I headed for the garage exit. I rarely ventured above Centre Avenue garage, where Yellow had its offices and radio room, as I had a clean record with few complaints, and zero at- fault accidents. I started up the steel, fire-escape style staircase hugging the side of the building…

...and stopped. Froze. One foot on the second step, the other on the third. I could not move. Or even think. Shut my eyes. For how long, I'll never know. Thirty seconds? Three minutes? Five? More? I'll never know if any fellow members of the human race took notice of my prolonged statuary position at the foot of a steel stairwell. If so, I guess I looked pretty stupid.

Finally, after *X* amount of time, I unfroze, looked around, and took a deep breath. And came to a resolution: *Fuck it—I'm good!* I reversed my stair climb, turned around, and walked away. Not forever. As the men in the cage always say, "They all come back, they always come back." I gathered my thoughts; I needed a break from this. But I would come back. Next week? Maybe around Thanksgiving? After Christmas? I'll just go to the paper pushers upstairs and get a return slip. I remembered my previous off and on privileges from my part time college days with my union withdrawal card and smiled.

The days became weeks. The weeks; months. Months turned into years. But life was good. As time passed, I was able to pick better turns with daylight hours at the bus company, we got yearly pay bumps, and more vacation time. The job still sucked, but no complaints.

But there was this itch. I missed the hustle; the risk taking. I even missed the road! I still worked overtime, but too many hours locked inside Port Authority's cages made me restless. I was never cut out to be an office person. But it wasn't time to return to the cab—not just yet.

Contrary to popular belief, the gig economy thrived for years before Uncle Uber's big idea mesmerized the world.

Taxi leasing has been around for decades. And there were others. It was time to seek them out.

***

Starting in 2003, for the next five years, I enslaved my personal vehicles into the world of independent contract delivery. I worked for—never as an employee—companies with names like *Time Pro, Wes Pax, The Expediters;* I was even an *Office Boy,* even though my car was my office. I delivered everything from blood to lab work, medical supplies, pharmaceuticals, paper, legal documents, computer parts, transplant organs—even a pancreas! One time, I delivered caged birds from the airport to a pet store in Ohio and swore they were singing in harmony with the chorus to The Beatles song, *I'm Looking Through You,* I had playing. Around Mothers Days and Valentines Days, I arranged a gig with a local florist. I did not mind burning vacation days for those, as it meant big bucks—plus, my car smelled nice for a couple days.

And there was luggage. Tons of lost baggage. Did the airlines ever lose your checked bags only to have a guy show up with them at your house or workplace the next day? That may have been me. You'd be amazed how much a Taurus wagon—I destroyed that—or a Subaru Outback could haul. The lost luggage became my main side gig. There were two competing companies that covered all the airlines between them, and I delivered for both simultaneously. I relished the challenge of finding obscure addresses in the middle of nowhere, without GPS, and was at peace blasting my favorite tunes. I even delivered to some of the bus operators I worked with a few times. And there was no better tip than a ripe pineapple, fresh from Hawaii. I began wondering if I preferred the company of cargo to people, or was I simply allergic to humanity?

***

January 2008

Wow—allergic to humanity! I've often thought of myself as "not really a people person" while some who know me well would take issue with that.

I was still doing *the airlines lost my luggage thing,* and just—(celebrated?) my tenth year with my employer. It felt like a lifetime ago since I stood catatonic at the foot of the stairway to Yellow Cab's heaven. When I finally unfroze and left the property, six weeks, maybe even a six- month hiatus crossed what remained of my mind. It was now north of six years.

One thing I never understood about delivering luggage was that very few people ever tipped. You would think people would be thrilled to be reunited with their stuff. The few who did tip usually tipped well, often a ten, or twenty, one time a fifty. I suppose most people thought we were airline employees who somehow were responsible for their inconvenience. Or were they happier to see the pizza guy at their door than the one with an oversized suitcase containing dirty underwear? The non tipping, the wear and tear on my cars, plus my aching back, made the lost luggage gig feel stale. And every time I arrived and departed from the airport, it was hard not to notice the steady yellow parade dropping off and picking up people, knowing 99% of them were tippers. I missed that life, recalling the airport as The Promised Land. It was time.

Six years can seem an eternity. It was not a matter of simply going upstairs for paperwork. There was, in fact, no more upstairs. The Centre Avenue garage succumbed to East Liberty's gentrification, supplanted by a Whole Foods anchored retail development. Yellow Cab Company consolidated all operations to their North Side facility.

I reapplied, letting them know I was driver 9694. They had no record of me. Erased—a new identity ordered. My third life in cab-land; just call me 6311. They scheduled me for "training." Unpaid, for a week! The other two times I was indoctrinated it was one, then two days. I didn't want to burn vacation days this early in the year, but I wanted to be back in the game.

My job at Port Authority involved coordinating all operators' vacation time at my division, Harmar, which I endeared as *Saint Harmar*, to my boss's chagrin. The Friday before my training, Mike, one of the bus operators, requested a day for that Monday. No problem. I reported at 8 AM sharp on a brisk Monday morning; of course, the building with the training room was locked, and we had to wait twenty minutes in the cold for someone to show up. There were three of us. Me, this other guy, and guess who—Mike, the bus driver. We both got a chuckle from that.

Mike, it turned out, already drove for Yellow. However, the one lease per month minimum rules still applied, and Mike missed a few weeks and needed to be "retrained." Fortunately, the instructor was a man named Eric, who began his taxi career in the 1980s and used to pick my (limited) brain for advice. Mike only had to do one day; Eric let me graduate after two. The third person had to run the gamut, I guess.

And, of course, good-old Fred, who handed me my first manifest thirty years earlier, was still in the cage. And repeated his mantra. "They always comeback, they just keep coming back!"

It was nice to be home again.

CHAPTER 26

Fire and Rain

Christmas Eve Eve – December 23, 2008

At Christmastime, not everyone has a ride. Or even a place to be.

As independent contractors, taxi drivers have a choice to work or not, and the vast majority opt for a well- deserved and much needed hiatus from cab life for this holiday week. And for the first time after eleven years of employment at Port Authority, my departmental seniority enabled me to schedule Christmas week off.

It was no easy decision to pass on the trip to South Jersey with the family for the annual holiday thing. With a thick pile of bills and a week away from the real job, I decided to spend this "vacation" doing what workaholics do. My winter solstice would be devoted to patrolling lonely streets in a yellow for hire vehicle.

Upon my midafternoon arrival at the garage, it was no surprise to find the yard overflowing with empty cabs. The

199

plan was to find a good one to hold down for a few days. Parked in front of a row close to the gate calling out my name was cab number 533, an immaculate, new to the fleet, Ford Crown Vic ex police cruiser. My old buddy, Henry, was manning the cage and happy to honor my request, especially after a cleaned and pressed twenty- dollar bill slid through the small window slot, wishing him a holly-jolly Christmas.

This was not my first rodeo celebrating Christmas inside a motorized yellow companion, so I knew to curb any lofty expectations. With most of the normal populace taking a rest from work or school, business would be light, at times dead; traffic would be light—not a bad thing, and competition would be light—a good thing. The strategy was to chase after any call within reason, and not outthink myself, as I am so prone to do.

By seven o'clock, with just four short, shitty trips under my belt, I recalled the fourth law of Christmas Cab Science— shitty tips. People would expect this to be the best tipping week of the year, but the opposite is most often the case. During the holiday season, through the weeks leading up to the big day, tips can be spectacular. As Christmas closes in, the tipping tends to dwindle. Throughout December, people attend lavish holiday parties, exchange presents, receive company bonuses, and so forth. As the holiday itself comes nigh, the credit card bills show up as well as the relatives who, thank the lord, only appear annually. Add in the gloom of the shortest, darkest days of the year and chronic grumpiness sets in—no tip for you! Of course, none of this has ever been empirically documented or researched, they are only theories from this deranged and crabby cabby.

With only myself and three cats at home—yes, I fed them that morning—I headed for *Mineo's Pizza* in Squirrel Hill, as I could hear the voices of two slices with mushrooms inviting me for dinner. We all hear voices from time to time, but not from cars or carbohydrates. I began to second guess my decision to not take an actual vacation during my vacation.

I returned from my pizza feast to find a dispatch screen devoid of anything resembling a request for a taxi. I called Chris in New Jersey to verify their safe arrival, now super pissed- off at myself for wasting away in a large yellow Ford instead of joining my family. While some folks have no place to be on holidays, others choose to be alone. People need rides. Cats need food.

For a good twenty minutes, I sat without a fare close enough to chase, wasting precious fuel, contributing to global warming. It was not freezing, but chilly enough to need the heat. A trip in Zone 400 popped onto the screen. This zone encompasses Homestead, a proud rust belt town across the Monongahela River bordering the city's edge. The bulk of calls in this area come from The Waterfront, a pseudo- Disney-like complex of big box retail, trendy dining, and entertainment rising from the ashes of what once was the world's most productive steel mill. A smaller percentage of trips in 400 were in real world Homestead, still struggling to recover from the economic downturn of the 1980s. I banged the 400, what did I have to lose? Looking up at the clear winter sky, I shut my eyes and wished upon a star for a trip from a Waterfront hotspot, perhaps a company's late holiday party. My imaginary rider enjoyed some fine liquid spirits and was in a jovial spirit at tipping time, after a pleasant forty- minute highway ride to his suburban abode. I opened my eyes—back to reality. This order was in real world Homestead, in a hood up a hill. Oh well, this line of work has always been and will always be a dice roll. I proceeded towards East Sixteenth Avenue.

I climbed McClure Street, a steep road dissecting the numbered cross streets, and spotted a red, orange, and blue light show in the distance. What was I getting into, why was I out here at all? There had been a rash of recent shootings in the neighborhood, what was happening tonight? As I neared the flashing lights, the unmistakable stench of smoke filled the air. A flood of fire, police, and other emergency equipment populated the streets, blocking the intersection. A police officer motioned, directing me into a parking space across the street from a smoldering, damaged house. A Red Cross volunteer walked over to my driver's window, shaking his head, "we told them we needed a van cab. These people have a lot of stuff to haul!"

My first thought was *hey, I can get out of this!* Even though it was another step in an unproductive night of wasting time and gas, I really did not want to turn my cab into a moving truck. I glanced over at the postfire scene. First responders, bystanders, and the displaced family milled around the front yard and sidewalk near the house. Random stacked boxes, milk crates, garbage bags, and miscellaneous odds and ends were scattered about. *Oh wow, there's kids!* Three children huddled near the corner of the yard, including a shivering young girl, perhaps ten years old with a blanket wrapped around her, finishing a good cry.

I now felt like a total dick for even entertaining the thought of not trying to help these people. My attitude took an abrupt one-eighty. "Hey," I looked up at the flustered Red Cross guy, "I think we can handle this. The cab company probably didn't have any vans available, but these Crown-Vic's have enormous trunk space."

Mr. Red Cross nodded in agreement, "Let's give it a shot." As I stepped out of the car, he handed me a clipboard with an attached taxi voucher to sign. The fire victims, a sixtyish African American couple approached, the woman offering profuse gratitude for my simply showing up. A younger woman, probably a relative, arrived at the same time to take charge of the children, who I later learned were the couple's grandchildren and teenaged nephew.

The gentleman expressed doubt that we could get all their salvaged belongings into the cab. I recalled my previous side job of delivering the airlines' misplaced baggage. With creative ingenuity, it was amazing how many suitcases, golf bags, duffle bags, and boxes could be stuffed into an old Subaru Outback. The challenge was on, I was all in. "Where there's a will, there's a way. We can do it!"

A couple of neighbors, Red Cross folks, and some of the firemen helped lug the cargo from the front of the house to the taxi. I loaded and stacked, using every available space the cab had to offer. There were plastic bags full of clothing, boxes packed with dishes, milk crates stacked with photographs and memories. Some of the stuff reeked of an after-the-fire, acrid, chemical smell, but I resigned to calling it a night after this trip and allow the winter air to wash away any aftermath. Within fifteen minutes, we were all loaded. The trunk was barely able to close, the front passenger seat and floor were stuffed, with just enough space to squeeze the couple into the back seat. While they were able to salvage some items, the man said most of their furniture and appliances were destroyed as well as several irreplaceable, sentimental items.

The Red Cross arranged lodging at a nearby Holiday Inn, the one in Braddock Hills, less than a fifteen- minute ride. This was good for me, as it was only three miles from my home, and I planned to end my night anyway. I tried not to think about the irony of these poor folks spending the holidays at a Holiday Inn under these circumstances. There was nothing festive about their predicament. Would a Comfort Inn have been a better idea?

Normal taxi small talk was not the prescription for this night. The short ride was a quiet one, interrupted by the only clichés I could muster—*Thank G-d everyone was safe...You can always replace stuff...It will all work out.* None of this would improve their situation.

It required four luggage carts to wheel the family's leftover treasures through the hotel lobby to the elevators. They thanked me again and I wished them a Merry Christmas. When I returned to the cab, I wondered whether that was the stupidest thing I could say to someone in that moment.

I drove straight home, leaving the taxi'swindows open overnight, despite the frigid air. Combined with an aggressive dose of *Fabreeze New Car Scent,* the bitter cold chased the burnt funk away from the cab's interior into the wintery gloom.

***

Christmas Eve

At least my cats were pleased to see me, especially when rewarded with the sounds of the pull tab from a can of *Friskies*. It was just past nine thirty, way too early for bed. I settled into my recliner with the remote, "my friend," as my thirteen- year- old, Rachel nicknamed it. There was nothing exciting on tv, so my friend and I channel surfed through tired Christmas specials while awaiting the eleven o'clock news.

I expected the Homestead inferno to be the top story, but it only earned an honorable mention along with a brief cameo of flashing firetruck lights; nothing to see here. After nodding off in the recliner, I woke up about three AM, took a quick shower and dragged myself to bed. Around five in the morning, there were barely audible sounds of distant sirens, which I thought nothing of as I re-closed my eyes and returned to dreamland.

After waking up, I dressed and jumped into the cab, heading to McDonald's for a coffee and *McMuffin*. The cab was freezing, but the char-broiled memories of the previous night's work had dissipated. Following breakfast, I decided to hang out with my cats before embarking on a lonely Christmas Eve of cabbing. Upon reunification with the recliner, I pressed the power button on my friend to catch the noon news.

The newscast teased with the expected hoopla of Christmas Eve, but the top story was too close to home—not just in a geographic sense. The televised newsfeed involved a cluster of fire equipment from multiple departments. This was not last night's Homestead incident. I recalled those faint early morning faint sirens, but this was not a fire— quite the opposite, in fact. The fire engines filled the driveway of a large hotel. A Holiday Inn. *Oh, shit!* It was *that* one, the one in Braddock Hills.

A frozen water line burst overnight on the top (eleventh) floor of the hotel, spilling a steady torrent of icy water through the entire structure. Every floor, every room, the kitchen, the bar, restaurant, the entire lobby flooded. There were no reported drownings, no one died. Several guests slipped and fell while being evacuated, but there were no serious injuries. The reporter interviewed a hotel staffer who estimated that it could take a month or two to clean up, repair the damage, and reopen. A fire captain on the scene was less optimistic, expressing grave concerns regarding the integrity of the building, and mold damage. It was a Christmas Eve mess.

The reporter stated there were only a few dozen guests that night in the large hotel, who he described as "fortunate." He interviewed a young couple who took the whole thing in good spirits, because while all their packed clothing got soaked or damaged, they now had a story to tell. Almost all the hotel's furniture and fixtures were drenched, destroyed, as well as many of the guests' material possessions. The couple from the fire did not make it on the newscast for this story. But...there was a light at the end of the tunnel! The Holiday Inn arranged to transfer the remaining guests to—you guessed right—another Holiday Inn. What a... holiday?

I wasn't there, but surely somebody outside the swampy lobby of that hotel, perhaps a fellow traveler, a hotel manager, an empathetic first responder, assured my previous night's passengers as I attempted to… *At least everyone got out safe… You can replace your things…It will all work out.*

Smoke. Fire. A home annihilated. Memories destroyed. A few mementos were recovered. Preserved. Transport to shelter. A safe, warm place to stay. Sleep… A deluge of ice water. Panic. Escape. Destruction. More loss. Christmas Eve!

The Braddock Hills Holiday Inn never reopened. After ten years of back and forth between concerned parties over whether to demolish or sell the building, it was repurposed as a moving and storage facility. Hopefully, the water lines are sound.

I don't know what became of the family, but sometimes think of them when driving past the old Holiday Inn, with sincere hopes of their subsequent holidays being kinder. At other times, I remind myself that my own life has not been all that bad.

And my cats? They don't know how good they've got it.

Spoiled brat cats.

CHAPTER 27

G 20

September 2009

I t was, for sure, to be a momentous happening—the world coming to Pittsburgh! A who's-who extravaganza of presidents, prime ministers, royalty, diplomats, and renowned economic scholars converging upon our little town. Although there were initial whispers of the preferred gathering place being The Big Apple, President Obama somehow steered the annual G-20 summit to the 'Burgh, of all places. Our time had finally come to shine, the secret would soon be out. Our transformation from a Rust Belt relic to a dynamic, thriving hotspot was to be the news of the world.

With few exceptions, major conventions are reliable gold mines for cab drivers and service industry workers. Some conferences, like religious themed, multi-level marketing schemes, or worse yet, a cult-like combination of those— think Amway—often wind up as financial duds for the tip dependent workforce of the host city. But the G-20? This was a once-in-a-lifetime opportunity; the movers and shakers of the world's biggest economies descending on *us*—wow! What could ever go wrong?

The meetings took place on a Thursday and Friday, September 24th and 25th. With several unburnt vacation days from job number one, I thought what a great idea it was to take a break from work by working elsewhere, the pretzel logic of a workaholic. Maybe I should have taken the hint when my weekday cab partner said he wanted nothing to do with the G-20 and offered me the cab for the whole week.

Yes, I heard the forecasts of chaos, anarchy, protests, even violence. I could live with that, maybe even learn from it. I was not about to let a few dissenters get in the way of my big money- making opportunity. And surely the local powers-that-be would never allow out of town agitators and anarchists to shut down this great city. Why would they ever let that happen when they can simply screw it up on their own?

The week kicked-off with glimmers of hope, as flocks of corporate, diplomatic, and media A-listers from every continent—Antarctica notwithstanding—flocked into town for the big event, triggering a frenzy of rides to town from The Promised Land, along with the expected bar hopping, cuisine sampling, and occasional strip club scouting intrinsic to most major gatherings. A cabbie's dream!

The wake-up call came abruptly. By Tuesday, things started to unravel. Downtown office workers were told to stay home for the rest of the week, schools and businesses closed, the bulk of the restaurants—even Downtown, where the action was to be, shut down. Concrete barriers popped up everywhere, blocking streets, bridges, even sidewalks. By

Wednesday morning, not only downtown, but most of the surrounding neighborhoods, especially near the universities, were militarized. Thousands of police and National Guard were imported to "secure" the city. All 900-plus Pittsburgh officers were mandated to twelve- hour shifts, supplemented by every overlapping law enforcement agency, including the county police, sheriff's department, Port Authority, Pitt, CMU, Duquesne campus police—you get the idea. If that wasn't enough, dozens of Pennsylvania state troopers, police from almost every suburban department in this county of *only* 130 municipalities, even cops from Baltimore, Chicago, and New York poured into our big, small town. Armored vehicles, horseback patrols, military convoys, motorcycle cops, and a fashion show of riot gear filled the streets, outnumbering civilians in some areas twenty to one. Helicopters buzzed everywhere, at times dangerously low to the ground. And the conductor of this authoritarian orchestra was, at least in theory, The United States Secret Service! I did note several suspicious looking guys lurking around, who looked like a humorless version of The Blues Brothers.

And—my brilliant plan to work the cab? Not too bright, not at all. Everything died, it was a virtual lockdown. A pandemic prelude, perhaps? Taxi business was slow. Painful. Yes, there were all these important people in town, but they were sequestered into a small, restricted area, unless they had special or media access. The bulk of the restaurants that chose to remain open reported having almost no business at all. Even the Greyhound Bus Terminal was blocked off, the busses diverted to McKeesport, a rust belt city that has never had a taste of the revival Pittsburgh enjoyed. I wound up with a couple of decent rides, as McKeesport is a good twelve miles from downtown. Perhaps the event planning professionals were not receptive to the idea of long- distance bus riding folk mingling with the rich and famous.

As dystopic as our world had become, I had my moments. There was an interesting short ride with a black-clad "protester" who could only say he was against "big government and stuff." He was friendly and respectful, even though he swore my name was *Dude*. My most memorable ride was with a Japanese journalist who I drove around for a couple of hours. His piece was about the city and its rebirth from an industrial, smoke- filled town to the center of commerce, education, medicine, and technology it was now purported to be. He specifically wanted to visit revived mill sites which were reconstituted into meccas of retail, entertainment, and robotics, and appreciated my knowledge of the history of those places.

While he was impressed with the modern, though gentrified, living quarters popping up in former brownfields, I thought it was fair and important for him to see the other side of the shiny object. He agreed to take a ride through some of our less "cosmopolitan" neighborhoods which do not typically attract tourists. We took a jaunt through Hazelwood, where J & L Steel once provided hundreds of great jobs and fed dozens of family businesses. As a normal, prideful Pittsburgher, I showed him where this and that *used to be*. He tipped quite well and had a photographer take a picture of he and I with the cab for his article.

Another of the few fond memories I will never forget, at least pre-dementia, was observing a— battalion? —of State

Police marching in a double column formation along Forbes Avenue. It was impressive to see their precision and discipline. When the commanding officer signaled an abrupt stop in front of Jimmy Johns Sandwich Shop, they removed their hats and single-filed, turned and continued in formation into the lunch spot. Hey, we all must eat!

The G-20? I don't know; resolutions were voted on, deals were made, treaties discussed, international relationships affirmed, economic theories proposed. I wonder how the attendees could have enjoyed our city without meeting its people or visiting our neighborhoods. Did they learn anything surprising or unique about us? Hopefully, they at least came away realizing that our version of Pittsburgh is spelled with an *h*.

And, as expected, there was anarchy. Broken windows. Graffiti. Riots. Violence. Tear gas. Rubber bullets. They even unveiled a fresh, new military/police state technique called Long Range Acoustic Device, which produced an unbearable blaring, piercing noise worse than a screeching hyena scratching a chalkboard. I suppose that we should have been honored to be the test town for that. There were arrests, many justifiable, many perhaps not. On Saturday, after most of the conference attendees were long gone, police rounded up Pitt students at random for the crime of—I still don't know. Leaving their rooms?

Conventions? Sure, bring us your teachers, bridge engineers, librarians—now there's a party crowd, believe it or not. Arts festivals, body builders, steelworkers, accountants, unions, car shows. We love you all! The G-20? G-7? Any cousins they may have? Uh, thanks. But no thanks.

CHAPTER 28

Almost Famous

July 2010

I settled into the first spot on the Westin Convention Center's feeder line on a mundane Friday afternoon. Few fares populate the MDT screen, not atypical for July 4th weekend. Not feeling particularly frisky, I will simply park here, read the paper, and witness the world stroll past until summoned by a passenger or doorman.

People wander along Tenth Street and upon the hotel property. A trip to The Promised Land seems unlikely, as most of the businesspeople already departed to begin their long holiday weekends. One constant among the passersby were hordes of tourists decked out in light blue or red and white pin-striped baseball shirts sporting a large red slanted *P* in honor of our cross-state rival Philadelphia Phillies. They are here for a four-game series, which prompts an impressive, annual migration of eastern Pennsylvanians westward to the 'burgh. We welcome the company; we really are friendly folk.

Turning to the sports section of *The Pittsburgh Post-Gazette*, I bypass articles most normal people would find intriguing, flipping instead to the baseball box scores.

Since grade school, I have been a Pirates fan and baseball fan. I also have forever been a numbers nerd, all excellent prerequisites for owning a fantasy baseball team. I unexpectedly stumbled into that world in the late 1980's, when fantasy sports were in their infancy. This was during my Greengrocer entrepreneurial years, when life revolved around things like strawberries, beets, cauliflower, and eggplant. Chris and some of our workers encouraged me to find a hobby, something to give my mind a break from fruit, and improve my mental well-being. Nancy, a Carnegie-Mellon art student, was married to Rob, a CMU grad student who commissioned something called a *Rotisserie Baseball League*. Up to this point, I had only ever associated that word with chicken and thought it was the stupidest sounding thing I had ever heard. Nancy told me that one of Rob's players departed Pittsburgh for a job in the real world and they needed another player to form a team.

Following days of convincing and salesmanship, I figured, "What the heck, why not?" I attended the league's draft, feeling completely out of place in a small apartment filled with Carnegie-Mellon computer and engineering geniuses, but successfully drafted my inaugural *Roto* league team. It was a challenging rookie season, absorbing the ups and downs and mastering the ins and outs of managing an imaginary roster of actual players and their real-time statistics. At seasons end, *The Parsnips* finished at a surprising and respectable third place in the highly competitive 10- team league. I was hooked!

I look up after five minutes of box-score analytics to finally observe some cab stand activity. A group of three men stroll over to the cab parked in the first spot on the stand. The man entering the left passenger side door looks exactly like Jimmy Rollins, Philadelphia's perennial All Star- shortstop. The Phillies and many of their fans encamp at the Westin for the weekend, not surprising given its reputation as a go- to hotel for visiting sports teams. As I angled into the first-up position on the cabstand, I noticed the other cab's right turn in the direction of PNC Park—probably was Rollins!

For fantasy baseball geeks like me, Jimmy Rollins is a well-known commodity, a universal first or second round draft pick. The only member of the Phillies I currently roster is their ace pitcher, Roy Halladay, who I would recognize anywhere. Hey, wouldn't it be cool if Halladay popped out of the hotel and took me over to the stadium? I've picked up both baseball and NFL players who were on my teams before but hesitated to inform them of their role in my fantasy life; they might have taken it the wrong way. If I picked up Halladay, I would at least let him know I am a fan of his, that I respect his game. Beyond that, I have been on this job long enough to realize celebrities, like the rest of us, struggle to make it through each day.

Besides the big names, I am familiar with 95% of all major league players. Our league is highly competitive, full of people with eons of fantasy baseball experience. We need to be knowledgeable of players from all levels to compete. It is a no brainer to secure superstars like Halladay and Rollins in the early part of a draft. The key to winning is to draft the sleepers, the players who were not on anyone else's radar. Some of the biggest impact players are drafted late, in the 19th or 23rd rounds, when empty pizza boxes and beer bottles litter the room. That is why serious fantasy gamer study practically every player. We could be sitting next to a random player in a bar, having a casual conversation, and have no clue that he's a ballplayer. Yet, upon hearing his name in passing, we would know he qualified at three infield positions and hit a pedestrian .262 with moderate power last year.

The familiar, loud verbal whistle from Mark, the Westin's Irish- born doorman interrupts my thoughts. Like any good cabbie, I respond promptly, pulling up to exactly where his hand meets the door. *Oh good-a tipper!* I note as the entering passenger slides Mark a couple of singles.

"Hi—PNC Park, players entrance," the man requests.

I nod, glancing into the mirror. A younger guy, even slouching in the back seat of the Impala, appears quite tall. I want to recognize him, but nothing outside of his height offers any clue. Maybe he is Ryan Howard's right-handed back up at first base, or perhaps a pitcher.

"So; how long have you played for the Phillies?" I immediately realize how stupid this question sounds after being tortured by *how long have you been driving a cab?* 50,000 times.

"Just got called up this year." He didn't seem offended.

It doesn't matter. I have driven more than my share of players over the years. Sure, it would be cool to tell people, hey, by the way, I had Tom Brady or Albert Pujols in my cab (I haven't), but there is nothing truly remarkable about it.

The thing that irritates me when pulling up to the stadium before the game, or even at the hotel afterwards, are those autograph hounds who swarm the cab to see who it is, barely allowing players a chance to breathe. Sometimes they are genuine fans, or young kids seeking to meet their heroes, but too often they are opportunists seeking multiple signatures to hawk online for profit. Even though some of these players make millions and it comes with celebrity territory, it is difficult to not empathize with them in these situations.

The trip from the Westin to the ballpark is a short one. As I turn left on Lacock Street, curiosity gets the better of me. "Hey, if you don't mind my asking, who are you anyway?"

"I'm Dave Herndon." Simple. To the point.

Wait, I'm stunned. As a professional fantasy nerd, I've never even heard of this guy! "Herndon? I never heard of you—what position do you play?" I look down, surprised to see my foot pressing the brake pedal when I feel like I just put it in my mouth.

Herndon sighs, "That's okay, a- lot of people don't know who I am. I'm just one of the bullpen pitchers."

I now feel bad for steering the dialogue to this level of awkwardness. "Man, I'm sorry, it's just that I play fantasy baseball and thought I knew all the Phillies." He chuckles. "I guess most people wouldn't have me on their teams. I'm the guy who usually comes in when the score is like 10-2."

"They used to call that the "mop-up man," I say.

"Something like that," Herndon laughs.

The traffic cop waves, approving my left turn onto Mazeroski Way. It looks like there are at least fifty people lingering near the player's gate. I can only imagine the throng of charging fans when Rollins' taxi pulled up a few minutes earlier.

I swing a quick U-turn, stopping near the entrance. The crowd immediately closes in, surrounding the cab. A chubby, middle aged man resembling Seinfeld's annoying neighbor, Newman, peers into the corner of the windshield, loudly announcing, "It's just Herndon." The crowd instantly dissipates.

Herndon hands me a crisp twenty. "Ten back would be fine."

I passed him back two fives. "Thanks; Hope you get in there and have a good game – as long as the Buccos win!"

Herndon smiles and exits, passing easily through the crowd. Nobody seeks David Herndon's autograph. Finally, as he nears the gate, a young boy runs up to him with a baseball. The player stops, happily fulfilling his young fan's wish.

The Pirates beat the Phillies that night. Jimmy Rollins did not get a hit in three times at bat, but David Herndon pitched a perfect inning of relief, striking out one batter.

David Herndon still never earned a spot on my fantasy baseball roster.

CHAPTER 29

Your Hailing Rulebook

March 2011

You are blinded by the expected yet abrupt disruption of the brightest lights on earth. It's closing time and the bar sends its not- so- subtle message. Glad you stopped by, hope you had a good time, thanks for spending lots of money, don't forget to tip your friendly bartender, now get the fuck out! You get the memo.

Scouting the room, you spot your two friends across the bar, raising your fist in victory while scribbling a ten- digit number provided from the hot, likely underage blonde who danced the night away with you, or at least the last fifteen minutes of it. A friendly pat-on-the back hug follows, allowing you to maintain the faint illusion of this being her actual phone number. You hook up with your party bros, Drew and Kevin, near the front doors. Kevin points across the room at your new friend with one hand while high fiving you with the other. It was a good night out. Good, not great. After all, you are leaving with Drew and Kevin rather than your sexy newfound friend..

"Dude—it's friggin' freezing out here!" Drew proclaims the obvious as your group merges onto the crowded sidewalk. It is 2:10 AM, time to find that elusive ride home. Hundreds of worn-out partiers flood the streets, the competition is fierce. There are occasional beacons of hope, lit taxi marquees scattered in the sea of traffic, nowhere near enough to gratify this crowd. And, honestly, forget your mom. She is sound asleep, and you're 27 years old, c'mon man! The three of you know the unspoken mission; find a taxi.

Although I am not driving one at this moment, please—allow me to help.

See that finely attired, still sober, attractive thirty-something couple in flagging mode, in front of you…yes, them. Just keep walking, you guys have zero chance in front of, behind, or around them. Distance yourselves.

"Hey, there's one!" Kevin notices the blatantly yellow Ford beast directly across the street. Problem? There are already four passengers inside, this cab's not for you. No one has ever accused Kevin of excessive brilliance.

A beat- up old Lexus with a yellow cardboard sign reading *CAR SERVICE* in the right corner of the windshield stops. Drew immediately goes for the jitney's door as you restrain him, recalling Rule #1: Don't get into unmarked cars with fake taxi signs. You'll likely get ripped off; worst case scenario, you may never be seen again. Look for actual cabs. You and Kevin pull Drew away, politely declining.

After another failed attempt, Drew shows signs of having consumed a beverage or two too many. An empty, bright yellow taxi stops, the driver nodding "hop in." Good ole' Drewster falls forward onto the front fender of the cab, spewing liquid venom. The cabby, understandably, locks the doors and peels away, shaking his head as he curses aloud with disgust. Rule #2: Don't vomit *on* the cab or you will never get the opportunity to vomit *in* the cab. Come on, guys, escort Drew to the nearest alley, let him get the rest out of his system. Clean him up the best you can, and please, insist on a complimentary breath mint; or, at least, a stick of gum.

Back to the task at hand—oh, great! Four young ladies who were apparent contestants in a shortest and lowest cut little black dress contest are competing right behind you. You have less chance now than you did with the dressed for success, sober couple. Rule #3: Any group of scantily attired women standing in the cold will always get a ride before you. Time to stake out a new spot…never mind, there are already two cabs claiming first dibs on the girls.

It's getting colder and you are feeling ever so desperate as the crowd has thinned out considerably. *"Dude!"* Drew points at an oncoming taxi. You moronically jump into the street, directly in the cab's path. The driver lays on his horn, narrowly missing you as his middle finger arises. Not your brightest idea. Rule #4: Never step in front of a moving vehicle. If the driver is in a bad mood or distracted state, you may become roadkill.

Drew feels more festive, now that all those undesirable fluids have escaped his system. As another taxi approaches.

Drew staggers off the curb, motioning back and forth, pointing his finger at the taxi as he screams, "You the man, you my man, you *da* man!" The driver shakes his head "no way" and keeps moving. A vacant cab behind him witnesses Drew's asinine antics and follows suit. Which brings us to Rule #5: Do not wildly gesture at a cabby while simultaneously complimenting him by yelling "You the man!" It will not get you a ride…unless the driver's desperation level exceeds yours.

Now it's up to Kevin. It is past 2:40 AM and the crowd has dissipated. Other people have successfully secured taxis while you guys are having no luck. A prospective cabby slows down, approaching with caution. Kevin, in full spaz mode, jumps up and down, frantically waving both arms, as if being pursued by a pack of hungry hyenas. The driver does an express risk vs. reward calculation, deciding thanks, but no thanks, once again passing you guys up. Rule #6: Do not perform crazy looking rituals as part of your taxi hailing behavior.

Hey, guys, I'm still here-hello? Here's free advice from my column, *Dear Cabby…*

You nod with approval, finally heeding my idea. Step toward the edge of the curb, your front foot on the street is fine. Your party bros stand behind you, acting calm. A cab is in view. Raise your preferred hand, attempting to make eye contact with the miserable bastard behind the wheel at 3 AM. A friendly face, with a not too pathetic *what about us* expression may be helpful. The cab pulls over and-*voila*-you guys found your way home.

Rule #7: Be polite. Treat the cab driver the way you would want to be treated. Try to not be a dick.

And, finally, Rules #8-9-10 and beyond: Please tip. And tip well. If you tip abundantly well, you may be rewarded with a cell number, a new weekend friend, and designated driver.

South Side bar crowd.

Woman gets the cab before You, Drew, and your drunk crew.

CHAPTER 30

Midnight Express

August 2012

I t's 11:44 PM on a hot, muggy Sunday night in the 'burgh. The ride in from the airport is quiet and uneventful. I confidently guess my passenger, a thirty-something, casually attired gentleman of Indian descent, is a "regular," an I.T. consultant commuting to his long- term assignment in the city, as he seems unfazed by downtown's reliably radiant light show as we spill out of the tunnels. His mind is elsewhere, while my tired brain contemplates my next move.

On Sunday nights, my routine is to turn in as close to 1:00 AM as possible, when the Yellow Cab's cage opens for business, although my weekend lease deal allows me to keep the cab out until 6 AM Monday, the time my day job begins. By the time I transfer my "cab stuff" from the taxi to my car, get the cab's fluids checked, wait in line, cash out, drive home, do paper- work, shower, and unwind, I am lucky to squeeze in two or three hours of sleep. I debate; should I take another shot at the 'port, or play it safe, run a couple of short trips, and call it a night? It had been a good evening, the airport gods were generous, this being my fifth trip in the past six hours.

As we pull in front of The Renaissance, I hear the ringer on my behind-the-times, yet good enough for me flip phone. A glance reveals Tony to be the caller. My passenger swipes his American Express, includes the predictable 15% gratuity, and we exchange pleasantries while I retrieve his proficiently packed carry-on from the trunk.

Jumping back into the taxi, I returned the call. "Was-sup, T. C., where ya'at?"

"Promised Land, third up downstairs, empty lot, flights on the ground... looks like a *blue light special* comin'—gotta go, got one!" Tony delivers the news I hoped to hear.

As the traffic light changes to an inviting green, I pound the gas pedal, hanging my left onto Fort Duquesne Blvd past the large, familiar road sign reading FORT PITT BRIDGE-AIRPORT.

11:49PM: I blast through the tunnel. I need to turn in soon, but cabby-hunger instinct once again overrules rationality. I seek another big score, just one last home run. The thrill of the chase strikes again as The Promised Land lures my return.

Shifting to the airport at midnight is a dicey proposition. Unless there are significant delays around the country, most flights have landed. Sundays, however, are the busiest nights at Pittsburgh International. Businesspeople arriving for their work weeks and Monday meetings, along with locals returning from weekend getaways pack the planes. I intensify my race out the Parkway West. High risk, high reward.

In the taxi, or any transportation industry, time means *everything*. It is an eighteen- mile ride from town to the airport with posted speed limits between 55 and 65 mph, but the roads are nice and dry; my license to fly. With an empty backseat and open highway, 75 to 85 mph becomes cab driver protocol. And, at this late time of night, a couple of competitors beating me to the punch could equal a world of difference between a quick turnaround or getting stuck without a trip.

11:57 PM: The final five- mile homestretch is a wide-open, six lane divided highway. With the speedometer pushing 85, my adrenaline synchronizes with the speed. Approaching McLaren Road, the final exit before the Airport Exit, I observe two sets of headlights invading my driver's side mirror. Within seconds, a two- car train of yellow Crown Victorias, topped with lit shark fin taxi marquees rumble past, no doubt exceeding 100 mph. This pisses me off, but I decided to not challenge these morons. The Pennsylvania State Police, who patrol this road, have always been tolerant with us. Chances that the radar guns are around at this moment are slim. But I would have no sympathy, perhaps a hint of satisfaction, if I passed the two clowns pulled over at the next exit in the shadows of flashing reds and blues. There has always been an unwritten, albeit unenforceable code of etiquette—even cabbies have their mannerly moments—that we don't pass each other on the final five- mile stretch when shifting. Unfortunately, in the ever-devolving taxi world, courtesy and protocol have been relegated into some future *Taxi Memorabilia Museum*.

MIDNIGHT: My heart pounds with anticipation as the arrowed *AIRPORT* road sign flashes by the right corner of my windshield. The two speed-racers are out of sight. I hope for a trip, preferably to…the telephone interrupts my racing thoughts. Tony just dropped off in town and needs an airport update.

"Just split the eagles, call you right back." I respond. The exit ramp transforms into a multilane boulevard, graced by dissecting, concrete pillars topped with impressive monuments of the majestic birds, serving as the airport's welcoming committee.

I continue to the holding lot, where commercial transportation vehicles segregate from the public. The clock reads 12:01 AM; I pat myself on the back, "Good timing." There are several limousines, a parking shuttle, a Super Shuttle van, but not a single cab in sight. I speed through the near empty lot, my wish fulfilled: *The blue light special!* A bright, high wattage, flashing blue light near the exit gate signifies that cabs are needed at the terminal-*NOW!* I speed-dial my buddy, "Put it in gear and go—waiting loads!"

"Thanks, already hitting the tunnels," Tony replies.

12:02 AM: Approaching the taxi stand, there is only one other cab, likely part of the duo idiot train that whizzed by minutes earlier. The driver appears not pleased, as he loads multiple pieces of oversized luggage. A surprisingly, orderly line of at least thirty patient travelers awaits. A group of three step forward from the front as I hop out to greet them. "Hi, hope you all didn't have to wait too long." What I conveniently omit is how happy I am that it was *them* waiting for *me* rather than *me* waiting for t*hem.*

A middle-aged, George Clooney look-a like is accompanied by two women, an attractive, well dressed Black woman in her forties, and a much younger, wide-eyed blonde who appears not far from fresh out of college. I open the back door for the ladies, then wheel their luggage to the trunk. "George's" Samsonite is perfectly packed, as is the older of the two female's designer floral-patterned carry- on bag. The younger lady seems to have packed her life away, her over-sized red suitcase weighing somewhere north of fifty pounds, coupled with a stuffed matching-colored backpack. It is easy to conclude that the Clooney-clone and African American lady are seasoned business travelers, while the younger one needs serious travel training. I inwardly chuckle, recalling a recent George Clooney movie with a similar dynamic.

The man sits shotgun while his traveling companions set-tle into the comfort of the back-seat. Before I even ask, Cloo-ney answers; "Marriott-Cranberry Woods." I was hoping for another simple trip back to town. But I smile. Cranberry is not a bad trip, one of my favorite destinations from the airport. It will put me a few minutes behind my 1:00 AM goal, but that's okay. The ride to Cranberry, a bustling, populated township due north of Pittsburgh, is an easy ride on a clear night, all interstate driving. We pull away as the driver of the front taxi slams his trunk—he looks pissed, for some reason—and a parade of five more cabs pull in to service the growing queue of tired travelers. My timing was perfect, good call.

The ride to Cranberry went smoothly. I keep the cab's speed in the mid- 70s range, as I seldom exceed 80 mph with live cargo on board. Clooney reclines in the front seat, closing his eyes, collecting his thoughts. My theory about the young-er lady rings true, as I overhear her express anxiety about their presentation to Westinghouse in the morning. The clearly more experienced female traveler offers reassurance and confidence boosting advice to her colleague. Oblivious to the ongoing dialogue, Clooney's head is at one with the passenger side window, snoring softly enough not to annoy, while sparing me from midnight small talk.

12:37 AM: Clooney awakens as we stop in the hotel's brick driveway, while his lovely colleague swipes her credit card as her junior co-worker looks on with apparent amazement. Her virgin cab ride, perhaps? I passed back the meter receipt to be signed; she seems satisfied with the service. The meter reads $92, and she selects the 25% tip option, bumping up the sale to a generous $115 and change. I thank her so much as she passes back my clipboard with the slip, even adding a smiley face as a small bonus. The smile makes my night.

1:14AM: I finally hit the taxi yard, ready to bid farewell until Friday to my yellow partner-in-crime. Although I know I should not care, I can't resist wondering, "Where did those two morons who flew by in such a hurry end up?"

Shifting to the 'port.

Splitting the eagles.

CHAPTER 31

Brad

February 2013

With growing impatience, I paced alongside the cab outside the rear emergency room entrance at Western Psychiatric Institute and Clinic, awaiting my fare. Locally known as Western Psych, it was the recent tragic scene of a deranged gunman's rampage, which made national headlines. After a few minutes, the heavily bolted steel door unlatched, as an imposing, sizeable security officer emerged waving a taxi voucher.

"Brad?" I inquired, confirming I had the right patient.

"I'm Brad," the voice behind the guard groaned. A tall, lanky young man with uncombed dirty blond hair and several days' growth of facial scruff sauntered towards the taxi, his hand reaching into his shirt pocket. "Can I smoke?"

"Sorry, no smoking in the car," I replied, noting the security guard's eyeroll as he turned and disappeared into the building.

Wearing a look of dejection, Brad slumped into the back seat, clutching a hospital issued plastic bag containing the few possessions he checked in with. We were on our way to Resolve, a voluntary inpatient facility on the city's eastern edge.

"When we get there, you can fire one up before you go in; it's a pretty quick ride."

"Thanks dude, I understand why I ain't allowed to smoke in your cab," Brad said.

"No problem," I offered, hoping to cap the conversation.

Throughout the years, I've transported countless psychiatric patients. In my younger days, having an educational interest in psychology, I would engage them, try to learn who they were, absorb their sad stories. These days, I don't want to know, nor really care. Call it callous, call it been-there-done-that, call it insensitive, call it whatever you want. I often prefer the sound of silence, unless treated to that timeless tune on the radio.

The trip began with the awkward, yet acceptable quiet which typifies so many cab rides. Brad decided to shatter the silence. "I wish I knew how I got to this point, dude."

"Here we go again," I told myself.

"Yeah, I moved up here, I dunno, like, two years ago. I just graduated WVU, got a job and moved in with my girl-friend—she's from here. Everything was goin' great, life was perfect, until a month ago." Brad shut down, with a hopeless downward stare. The silence was no longer comfortable.

"So, Brad…where were you from before this?' I have never been the champion conversation kick-starter, but I so love local geography.

Brad refocused. "You probably never heard of it; Follans-bee, West Virginia."

"Sure, I know where that is, been through there a couple times." For whatever reason, I enjoy conveying to people my familiarity with their territory, their neighborhood, *their* turf. Perhaps this was my way of bonding within the often unremarkable, short-lived relationships which constitute taxicab rides.

Brad perked up, "Oh, wow, I'm surprised. Most people have never even heard of Follansbee!"

"So...what happened? You said things were great until recently..." I now was curious, even if uncaring.

"I...you know how life is. Everything was hunky-dory; I was makin' good money, we had a nice place, it was all good. My girl, Kaitlyn was her name...ya know, I moved up here for her..." Brad clammed up again.

I half-heartedly prodded, "okay..."

"Anyway, dude, a couple weeks ago, I get home from work and all her shit was gone. No note, no text, no nothin'. I come to find out that she moved in with her old boyfriend and was sneakin' around for like six months."

"Wow, that really bites!" came my lame response.

"I was in love with that bitch! I spent six- grand on a goddamn ring I was gonna give her that weekend, then this shit! I couldn't think straight, just quit goin' to work, ended up gettin' fired. When I tried to find out what happened, she never answered any of my calls, or texts, nothing." Brad's tired eyes moistened as he stared out the window.

I reflected to the emotional wreck I became so many years ago when a girl who I deemed the love of my life gave me the heave-ho. It was not until Brad leaned his right elbow on the passenger door's armrest that I noticed the deep red gashes peeking out from his bandaged wrist. As we turned into Resolve's parking lot, I felt relieved this cab ride was complete, yet with at least a smidgeon of empathy for this young man.

"Hey, dude, thanks for the ride; and for listening," Brad said as he opened the door.

"Good luck, buddy. I hope you get back on your feet." This time, I really meant it.

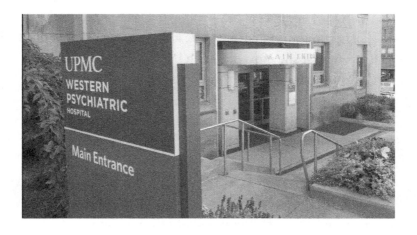

CHAPTER 32

Snow

Winter 1981/Spring 2013

The flurries began flying at dusk, harmless and sporadic, nothing to stop me and my yellow tank. It was Sunday night at the airport and visions of easy money swirled in my head.

Business was brisk at The Promised Land. As I started my second inbound trip, the winds kicked up ten notches, those lazy snowflakes became squalls, and the Parkway West transformed into an unsightly wonderland of untraceable tire tracks. In the back seat, Mr. Business Traveler wore an expression of pure horror, genuinely concerned about the prospect of safely reaching his destination.

I reassured him of my vast experience and total confidence in navigating these conditions and what a blizzard-proof vehicle the Checker was, none of which was a remote version of anything truthful. As conditions deteriorated, we persisted, the normal twenty- minute trip winding into a forty-five minute adventure. Upon our arrival at the warmly illuminated entrance of The Carlton House Hotel, my relieved and grateful client awarded me with an overly generous gratuity. The snowstorm intensified; the city streets were unrecognizable.

Naturally, I came to work unequipped with any semblance of a snow brush, ice scraper, or broom. I resorted to combining a cheap pair of cloth gloves with my jacket sleeves to clear the cab's windows the best I could. Should I return to the airport? I determined that most of my fellow cabbies would call it a night. My dad, who dreaded winter driving, would surely join that crowd. The choice was obvious; the only road to travel was the one returning to The Promised Land.

The violent winds intensified, knocking out power to streetlights and traffic signals. Few vehicles occupied the parkway, not one resembling a salt truck or plow. Even my 35- mph pace was too fast for circumstances, yet that did not stop at least six other taxis from leaving me in powdered dust clouds as if cruising on a spring-like morning. This job brings out degrees of insanity found in few other professions. I needed to hit that airport; people were waiting! Waiting loads translate into loads of money in my pocket. Oh, the greed!

The wipers barely kept pace with the battering sleet and snow. Sure, I white lied to Mr. Businessman about how terrific these taxicabs handled in a blizzard. With no weight in the back seat or trunk, combined with rear wheel drive and merciless crosswinds, the untreated highway was a terror to navigate.

There were only two traffic signals along the Parkway West between downtown and the old airport terminal. The first consisted of a single flashing light in a heavily wooded area at the dangerous T-intersection of McLaren Road. It reliably flashed a cautionary yellow along the highway and *don't even think about it* blinking red light facing the side road, forewarning unsuspecting motorists of this deadly crossing. Not tonight. "Holy shit, the lights are out!" I proclaimed to everyone within earshot—as in myself. When stress levels intensify, at times like this, I converse with myself. *Never seen it this bad... Should've quit while I was ahead... This really sucks...*

The other light, three miles down-road, was at the jug-handled exit ramp leading to the airport terminal, dissecting the four- lane divided highway. This intersection was normally well lit and heavily travelled. On this night, it was pitch black, no traffic lights. My internal solo dialogue resumed. *G-d, someone's gonna get killed out here!* I could barely see the outline of the roadways, let alone much else. As I approached the intersection crisscrossing the jug handle, a set of two red blinking lights barely pierced the near white out conditions.

"Hey, looks like the county cops got new hats!" I declared to my empty cab, noticing a lone figure in the middle of the blizzard infested roadway directing traffic, waving a flashlight. Allegheny County Police always wore rounded, gray trooper style hats; this one resembled a pilot's style hat, like those topping city officers, hotel doormen—even occasional old school cab drivers.

I impatiently finger drummed the steering wheel, anxious to be waved through. *How many can I squeeze in here?*

Maybe I can double, triple, hell, even quadruple up...come on, man, let's go ...

The flashlight motioned me onward. I felt sympathetic for the poor cop stuck on this detail on a night like...*Holy shit! That's no cop— it's Dad!* I stopped and cranked open my window, screaming into the storm, "What are you doing? Are you fuckin' crazy? You could get killed out here! There's got to be a hundred people at the terminal, you could clean up!"

He calmly nodded, saying, "Just be careful out here, son. These roads are terrible. Take your time."

I shook my head in disbelief, continuing to the airport's cabstand. Who in this world would risk their life in the middle of a blizzard to do someone else's job, foregoing all those waving twenty- dollar bills two minutes away? My father: good ole' Max, he was— different.

I pulled to an absolute mob scene, at least 150 people waiting for transit at the ground transportation terminal. I squeezed in seven people and their luggage, all heading in the same direction, with four separate destinations—a quadruple fare, a grand slam homer! The snow was relentless, but the added weight of the riders and their luggage made the trip easier. Each stop cheerfully paid full freight, all tipping abundantly.

Upon my return two hours later, I felt relieved to see two county officers in their familiar hats staffing the still lightless intersection. The snowstorm had eased. Max had done his duty, holding down the fort. I worked till three in the morning, bringing in a bundle of cash. When I encountered Dad the next day, he said he ended up with a decent trip after his voluntary traffic adventure and called it a night. I thought he was nuts and told him so.

***

Max Ehrlichman took his final breath on April 4th, 2013. He and I rarely hung out or had those extended heart to hearts, but it was a heartbreaking day. No words are strong enough to describe how painful it was to watch dementia overtake this remarkable, kind, and decent man.

His parents died early in his childhood, which he spent shuffling between foster homes and relatives. Before finishing high school, Max volunteered his services to the country he loved, fulfilling two tours of duty in Korea. While the scars of war haunted him throughout life, he rarely elaborated on the harshest parts of his service, instead fondly remembering his army buddies, and trading cigarette rations for beer. He kept an old cigar box full of medals and commendations, including his bronze star and purple heart. Max was wounded in battle, but the only detail ever offered was he was only doing his job. What he cherished most was the brotherhood between soldiers, the irrelevance of race, nationality, or religion, a theme he carried throughout his life.

Following the war, my parents married, raising three kids. We struggled financially for years, moving from apartment to apartment. My dad worked various jobs in the sixties and seventies, mostly as a Teamsters truck driver, delivering for local and national companies. In the early seventies, he began driving a taxi on Saturdays to help make ends meet, liking the job enough to eventually become a full-time Yellow Cab driver. And, thanks to a friendly loan through the GI Bill, he was finally able to purchase our family home, a modest but solid red brick in working-class Greenfield, where my parents encamped for the next forty years.

He was always a character, as one of a kind as ever was. In my younger years, I often referred to and addressed him as "Max" rather than Dad, even though he preferred the latter. I could author an entire book of "Max stories," each one funnier than the last, all barely believable yet true. My father and I were often worlds apart; we did not always see eye- to- eye, but I knew his heart was golden. Although I was an obnoxious and rebellious kid, especially in my early teens, my dad never put me down, never judged.

Max was never confused with the *Ward Cleaver* or *Mike Brady* image of a father, but he was a great dad in his own unique ways. Sometimes on the coldest or rainiest early mornings, he insisted on driving me around on my paper routes before he went to work. I never expected it, yet be-grudgingly appreciated it. Other times, he would go over-board, like collecting from my newspaper customers without my knowledge, encouraging them to pay a month in advance, with the faint hope of me using the resulting spare time to do things like homework; it did not usually work. When he did these things, always with good intent, I would sometimes make no secret of my outrage, routinely peppered with color-ful vulgarities, although I knew he was only looking out for me. Incidentally, unlike his middle child, Max Ehrlichman almost never swore. In rare instances of extreme anger, an occasional "damn it!" required an extensive effort.

Max had his causes. He passionately supported veterans of every stripe and the organizations that embraced them. When my siblings and I were in Hebrew school, he always found time to fundraise for *The Hebrew Institute Fathers Club*. And he was a proud and active union member, as both a truck driver and a taxi driver.

My dad was highly regarded by his taxicab passengers, earning the loyalty of a healthy roster of steady travelers who scheduled their airport rides exclusively through him. At times when he was double-booked or unavailable, I would back him up, keeping it in the family. Max's regulars always asked about him, universally expressing how much they enjoyed their rides to the airport—who else could brighten up your day at 4 AM? One of his frequent flyers, a likeable thirty-something family- man who I knew only as "Mike from Etna" always talked about how "cool" he thought my father was. Cool? I always thought of him as "uncool." But Etna Mike was right.

And there was Mr. Rogers. He was so polite when he called for my dad. "Good evening, this is Fred Rogers. May I please speak with Max?" The iconic, timeless children's television host's first choice for his neighborhood cab driver was none other than my dad. On the few occasions I had the pleasure of taking Mr. Rogers, or he and Mrs. Rogers to the airport, he always made it a point to ask about Max. Fred Rogers was every bit as sincere and genuine as the man who welcomed us to his TV neighborhood for years. The first time I picked him up, I was still a student. I wish I could recall his exact words as Mr. Rogers mentioned a previous ride with Max talking about how proud he was to have a son attend college. Mr. Rogers somehow steered our conversation, convincing me how fortunate I was to have a father like mine. Fred Rogers was also right; hey, he's Mr. Rogers.

***

I chose not to speak at Dad's funeral service, not that I had nothing to say, I am simply not a great eulogist. My siblings, Ben, and Linda recollected warm memories, while my oldest son, Justin pinch hit for me. One thing that Justin attributed to his grandfather was his strong work ethic and how he passed it on to the next generations. My friend, Bernie, rehashed a hilarious story about meeting my parents.

Until that day, I had forgotten about that snowstorm. Over the years, I worked through countless extreme weather events. While Bernie spoke, part of his story was when he was a little kid, remembering Max as the crazy guy running around selling raffle tickets wearing a Jewish War Veterans hat. At that moment, I closed my eyes, and recalled muttering these words: *Hey, looks like the county cops got new hats!*

It took over fifty years for me to get it, to capture who my father really was. He was the guy who put others first. On a miserable Sunday night in a blinding snowstorm, a man pulled over to the side of a road, stood in a dangerous intersection with a cheap flashlight, only to ensure that others didn't get hurt. He was only being who he always was.

"County cops got new hats?"

Mom and Dad

CHAPTER 33

The Holiday

Christmas Eve 2013

Everywhere, except here, holiday lights shine, candles burn, and the starry Christmas sky offers more than a glimmer of hope for the coming year. Festive evergreens and decorated Douglas Firs surrounded with meticulously wrapped presents radiate rooms as families and friends gather, sharing the warmest of greetings, telling wonderous stories. The holiday turkey sizzles to crisp perfection as new chapters of delightful memories unfold. Meanwhile, five lonely taxis idle in the frigid, near empty holding lot at Pittsburgh International Airport, their drivers awaiting their own Christmas dream. Or lack of one.

Braving the bitter winds, I pop open the trunk, scavenging the bottom of my lunchbox for any uneaten foodstuffs. A half of a slightly smashed salami sandwich, a bruised kiwifruit and a can of Diet Pepsi will make a fine meal. Starting the engine to catch a dose of heat, I take some paper towels from the glove compartment, creating an elegant holiday table-cloth over the center console to enjoy Christmas dinner; yes, this *is* the- life!

Time almost stands still, as each cab inches their way to the terminal taxi stand. Finally, after a near eternity, it is my turn to join the front four, the number of cabs permit-ted to stage at the ground transportation terminal. While the holidays are indeed a busy time for travel, they can be painfully slow for cabbies. By Christmas Eve, college students and faculty are long gone, while most business travelers have finished their year, embracing well-earned family time. Uncle Karl and Grandma will be greeted with hugs and kisses at the baggage claim by family members; few will need our services. I phoned Chris to say hi. Our four kids and my mom are at our home, enjoying the evening while I await my fate at The Promised Land.

As each taxi ahead of me receives its Christmas present from the airport, I move up until finally, I am *it*. First-up at the port! Every cabbie's dream- come- true. My mind wan-ders…*Man, a trip to Monroeville would be perfect right now! I drop them off, get maybe $90.00 plus a huge tip for my holiday sacrifice, go home, have some lasagna, unwrap…*

I depart my daydream, noticing potential customers approach. What will The Promised Land bestow upon me this cold winter night? Spotting a lady in an airlines provided wheelchair assisted by a US Airways employee, accompanied by a gentleman rolling two substantial pieces of luggage, I spring into action, hustling to open the trunk and rear passenger side door of my inviting yellow chariot.

"Merry Christmas Eve— and welcome to Pittsburgh!"
How corny I can be.

I perk with encouragement as the woman rewards the airline employee with a crisp ten- dollar bill. Her companion helps her into the taxi as I load the awkward, heavy bags into the Taurus's spacious trunk. After opening the left side door for the male passenger, I slide into the driver's seat, hoping to hear a desirable destination.

"Take us to the Wyndham Grande, Downtown—.and, please, if you would give us a good ride at the speed limit, I will take care of you."

Music to my ears, laced with multiple notes of caution. Often, people who *talk up the tip* turn out to be under average tippers, mediocre at best. Tonight, however, I have every reason to be optimistic. The handsome tip awarded to the airline employee was indeed a good omen, and after all, it is Christmas Eve!

"You got it," I reply. The roads are lightly glazed with freshly fallen snow, so I am not about to role-play Mario Andretti this evening. And, after a two- hour wait, arriving at the hotel Wyndham two minutes later will in no way alter my life.

The trip from the Airport to Wyndham Grande is a common tale for the average Pittsburgh cabby. One of the city's largest hotels, it is the first major landmark building visible upon exiting the Fort Pitt Tunnels as our magnificent skyline bursts into view.

"Driver, this is absolutely the cleanest taxicab I have ever ridden in," compliments the lady.

"Thank you, ma'am. My buddy and I, who share this cab, take a lot of pride in keeping it this way. Our passengers deserve nothing less than the best." *A little thick, I know, but I use it all the time.*

The conversation evolves to the usual cab chit-chat. The gentleman, it turns out, is a frequent guest at the Wyndham, involved in a major remodeling project for the hotel. The lady is from Florida, visiting for the holidays. By my guesstimate, the gentleman appears to be in his middle forties, while the lady looks somewhere north of sixty. I cannot quite ascertain the nature of their relationship. Is this his wife; mother; cousin; mistress; sister… dominatrix? Why should it be my care or concern?

We continue inbound on the near empty Parkway. The cab was recently serviced by Yellow for preventative maintenance, adding new tires and fresh fluids, running like a new car. Respecting the passengers' wishes, I maintain a perfect 65 mph, dropping down to the posted speed of 55 as we approach the city.

"You are a good driver," the gentleman says. "Last time we took a cab, the cab was filthy, the driver was from some damn island, yapping on his phone the whole way in some foreign language and drove like a maniac. I gave him a good tip, but he didn't deserve one."

"Uh, sorry about that. Most of our drivers are pretty conscientious." Little white lies are effective in certain situations.

I think about what pot-of-gold awaits at the end of *this* rainbow. This was the most perfect cab ride in the cleanest cab ever; plus, he was kind enough to tip the other driver despite poor service. At least he did not make the blatantly annoying comment I too often hear about how glad he was that I am white. Or American. Whenever people point that out, I take a moment and glance at the back of my hands, if only to verify whether it's still true.

We begin our descent down steep Greentree hill, into the awaiting mouth of the Fort Pitt Tunnels. As our perfect ride crosses the bridge, the city's breathtaking lightshow provides its reliable warm welcome. Seconds later, the taxi pulls to a safe stop in front of the Wyndham Grande's deserted driveway.

Bling! I cringe upon hearing the credit card being swiped on the *Taxi-Magic Machine* mounted on the back headrest. My holiday wishes included a cash trip, but we are regrettably becoming a cashless society. The hotel's doorman is on the case, opening the passenger door. While the credit card receipt slowly prints (my cab has the slowest printer on the planet), I unload the luggage as the lady *again* thanks me profusely for the excellent ride. Per my usual practice, I attached the credit card slip to my clipboard for the gentleman to sign. Upon reentering the taxi, I check the slip, noticing the tip to be exactly 15 percent (the lowest of three options Taxi-Magic offers, other than *other*), and shake my head without a shred of surprise or disbelief.

It is 9:30 PM. I need wake up at 5AM tomorrow for my "real job." Should I run another trip or two, in search of a cabby's better Christmas dream? Fuck it; time to call it a night. I drive towards the garage, parking the cab on a nearby street—I had married the cab for the entire week—and jump into my car to head home. Our family gathering is breaking up as I arrive, so I say a brief hello and goodnight to all, closing my eyes to yet another forgettable holiday.

CHAPTER 34

The Beginning of The End

May 18, 2014

Graduation weekend! For astute taxicab professionals, always one to circle on the calendar, especially Carnegie Mellon's commencement. At least it always had been. Countless travelers converge upon the 'burgh from across the country and around the world to celebrate this life achieving event.

The ceremonies occur on a Sunday morning in mid-May, rain, or shine, enveloped by numerous celebrations throughout the weekend. The airport always delivers on its unwritten promise in the days prior, while the city bustles all weekend with graduates and their guests shuttling about in hired yellow chariots.

Seasoned taxi-pro I think I am, I secure my cab for the weekend lease. Friday night and Saturday were, well, just okay, not quite decent. It seemed every cab in the county was on the streets, heavy competition. In addition, several weeks prior, the ride-share company, Lyft began operating, albeit unlicensed, in Pittsburgh. They were easy to spot, as the vehicles sported gaudy, oversized pink mustaches on their front grills. The mustaches were touted by some to be a concoction of clever, cool, and cute. I thought they were downright creepy.

To add to the mix, rumors circulated that a much larger taxi imitator, Uber, had also launched in the city. Business was tough enough; now everyone suddenly decided to become a glorified cabby. If the Uber rumors were true, they could be any other random vehicles, sans the obnoxious mustaches.

Following my ho-hum Friday and Saturday, I decided to start earlier than I would on a normal Sunday, around 9:30 AM. Routinely, I clean and air-freshen the cab's interior prior to taking any trips. I also stop at a local laser wash—at nine bucks, a justifiable business expense. On this special day, I make an extra effort, as I expect to transport well-attired clientele.

I headed directly towards the Shadyside and Squirrel Hill areas, which surround Carnegie Mellon (CMU). Business will be brisk. I could expect decent money shuttling people locally near the campus, and eventually seek out those important and inevitable trips to The Promised Land.

There were orders on the *MDT* board, but nowhere near the volume I projected. On a big day like this, I expect to easily cherry-pick an airport trip, or run several short trips per hour. Not today. It was busy, but I found myself with idle time in-between, more like a normal Sunday, certainly not graduation day! I observed quite a few pink moustaches moving about. This was strange, not like previous CMU commencements. Finally, after three hours of frustration, I locked in an order in Zone 305. Payday! Airport trip!

The fare was at CMU's University Center, a common pickup point. I hustled to get there, expecting to see more than a few taxis lurking around, some with legitimate calls, others looking to scoop up the first airport trip which happened by.

As I pulled into the University Center's large circular driveway, I noticed another Yellow Cab pulling away. Recognizing the driver immediately, I smiled and waved, knowing she was never one to steal a trip. There were other vehicles, some parked unsurprisingly half-assed, in the circle. I managed to secure a small parking spot, noting that I stood out as the only yellow car in the crowd. It was odd not to see other cabs sitting here on graduation day.

I called my customers, informing them I had arrived. They apologetically asked if I could wait ten minutes, as they had not expected service this quickly. I said, "Sure, no problem." If they were not going to the airport, I may have told them to call back when ready, but, man, I needed this trip.

It was a gorgeous afternoon, so this was a welcomed break, a chance to stand, stretch, and enjoy the sunshine. I was not exactly killing it business-wise but could not have asked for a nicer day. A steady stream of cars continued pulling into the circle, dropping off and leaving—nothing unusual here. Or... was there? At least a dozen vehicles were parked in the circle, more than usual, but this was, after all, the big day. As the SUV behind me pulled away, I glanced at a well-worn Chevy Cobalt parked behind him, its dirt-caked pink mustache staring back at me. A minute later, a newer, mustached

Toyota Camry discharged two ladies attired in colorful Indian Saris. I studied this unfolding, bewildering scene. Some cars seemed like they belonged there, while others looked oddly out of place. No hard science here; just old-fashioned cabby instinct.

A beater Buick Regal with obvious exhaust issues rumbled to a stop; probably a college kid dropping off his buddies. Wait a second—two dressed for success couples who looked like they returned from a snobatory country club emerged from the vehicle. The driver, an unshaven elderly Black gentleman, nodded goodbye. Forgive my lack of Kumbaya, but I did not take it he was giving friends a ride; he looked familiar—a jitney driver? As he pulled away, he honked and waved at a cigarette smoking man leaning against an Altima across the way. Uber? Am I dreaming—or is this my newest nightmare?

Ok, here we go, luggage; must be my trip! A couple hustled from the campus towards the driveway, each with a travel bag in tow. I jogged around the taxi, opening the passenger door and trunk. They suddenly stopped, about fifty feet short, as the woman became entranced with her cellphone. I turned to see the mustache-clad Cobalt abruptly pull out, stopping near the couple. The driver popped his trunk, like a taxi, loaded the luggage, the people, and took off. *What the actual fuck?* They were taking Lyft to The Promised Land!

I kept waiting, stunned by this eternal *oh- shit!* moment. Finally, three elegantly dressed people, a man and two women, middle- aged, strolled towards the cab. I loaded their bags as they thanked me repeatedly for my patience.

"Sure, no problem. Anytime!" We set out for The Promised Land. The ride to the airport; pleasant. The conversation; cordial. Their niece had just obtained her MBA. She was going places! The fare was good. The tip was fair.

As they vanished into the airport terminal, I had questions. *How big was this problem? Would there ever be another "anytime?"*

It was heartwarming to hear the young lady with the MBA was going places. As was the taxi business. Unfortunately, it was in the opposite direction.

Creepy mustache.

CHAPTER 35

Techno-Jitneys

June 2014

D espite the painful, clear-cut Uberization of the city that I knew and loved, I could not abandon my love affair with cabs. Not only in Pittsburgh, but across the nation, taxicabs are a relic of a bygone era. Reviled more than revered. Irrelevant. Obsolete. Within ten years, the sighting of a taxi on a city street will be viewed as quaint, like an Amish buggy, hopefully eliciting a fond memory or two.

From years of running a business, I grasped the importance of knowing and respecting the competition. Throughout my Greengrocer tenure, I made a conscientious effort to never badmouth my competitors. Having an intimate understanding of the taxi industry, it was difficult to have the same respect for Uber. On a level playing field, competition is a healthy recipe for companies and consumers alike, but the business practices of Uber and Lyft were deplorable—this playing field was anything but level. Now being aware of their impact, the logical next step was to research them, understand their operations.

I never encountered the word "rideshare" until the 2014 Pittsburgh mayoral race, when Bill Peduto, the current mayor, introduced his platform. It included a list of his positions on dozens of pertinent issues for the city, including transportation. Being immersed in both the bus and taxi industries, I was naturally curious about his ideas. The platform addressed taxicab issues in the city, such as a lack of available cabs on the streets and poor customer service—legitimate concerns! He advocated improving the situation by increasing the number of available taxis, establishing strategically located cab stands, and implementing something he called *ridesharing* in Pittsburgh. Mr. Peduto explained little about what rideshare meant, but it sounded like an excellent suggestion. My impression was it would involve innovative, nonprofit carpooling, which could ease congestion, and even improve our air quality.

Now a universally accepted term in the ever-evolving— not in a good way—English language, we all know what rideshare means. It sounds so warm and fuzzy, so Kumbaya. *Ride-share. The Sharing Economy. Your friend with a car.* It brings back memories from the innocence of early childhood television when Romper Room's Miss Jane, or the beloved Mr. Rogers taught us the inherent goodness of sharing with your neighbor.

In this Uber universe, I had difficulty contemplating this latest version of sharing. A driver shared her vehicle and labor, the passenger shared his money, while the Uber folks took more than their fair share of the fare from the driver's piggybank. All the while, Uber insisted it was *never* a transportation company, but merely an app bringing people together. It sounded no different than a glorified cab company to me.

Armed with this invaluable knowledge of the redefinition of the concept of *sharing,* I wanted to understand the rideshare culture. Justin, my oldest son, decided to drive Uber as a side job. He connected me with some Uber and Lyft drivers' Facebook groups. Up to that point, I had never been one to spend much time perusing the internet. Uber's explosion onto the scene rashly altered my secondary livelihood, and sadly, destroyed a way of life for many who relied on taxi careers to feed their families. Wanting to understand why, I monitored these sites, intrigued with the iconic taxi industry's nuclear level destruction by these sophisticated algorithms dispatching techno-jitneys.

Justin enjoyed his Uber adventures for a couple of months, but the novelty wore off. He benefited from some impressive and profitable nights, especially when *surges* kicked in. The surge, part of Uber's algorithmic pricing system, weighs supply verses demand. It evolved into an effective justification to gouge naïve riders into emptying their bank accounts, particularly at bar closing times. Justin showed me one fare where he netted $56 for a ride from Lawrenceville to West End, an easy, twelve- minute trip. This translated to a total sacrifice of over $70 from the rider to the gods of Uber! How much would the cab fare be? Between $16 and $18, on the meter, $20 with a respectable tip. For Justin, transporting entitled, intoxicated passengers who showed little regard for his vehicle became increasingly annoying, and he removed the black and white *U* logo from the corner of his windshield.

As I continued re-enlisting as a weekend warrior for Yellow, Uber persisted with its assault on the local market. At the time, neither rideshare company was licensed or insured to operate legitimately in Pennsylvania. I was baffled how people would pay three, four, sometimes five times cab fare to ride in unmarked, illegal jitneys. Uber's initial success was in large part due to the cab company's failure to provide reliable call and demand service. Now, I sat in my cab, trip-less on Saturday nights, observing car after car after car with pink moustaches and Uber stickers picking up and dropping off, one after the other. I felt humiliated.

Yet, I kept faithfully returning to the battlefield. In my antiquated canary colored tank.

A high Uber surge verses a regulated taxi ride. For a five-mile, fifteen- minute ride at the regular Uber rate calculated from this model, the fare would be a reasonable $14.00, approximately the same as the taxi would, based upon the above rate card. The Uber rate is only $1.25 per mile compared to $2.00 per mile for the cab. Uber charges per minute while a cab meter only registers time if the vehicle is at a complete stop for one full minute. Based on the above data, a base priced rideshare trip is virtually the same as taxi. However, at this moment in time, with the 8.9 surge in play, this ride will cost a hefty $114.50. Not a bad trip—for the driver. Note the one-dollar fee the rider pays for "trust and safety."

CHAPTER 36

Beaver Falls

July 2014

On a spring-like Saturday afternoon, after a couple of healthy, short trips, I snagged a decent one from Downtown to Pittsburgh Mills, a shopping complex in the distant northeast suburbs, for an easy $40. While there is typically not an abundance of business in that area, I always keep an open eye on the dispatch screen just in case. Usually, I inch back towards the center of taxi civilization without success. Upon hitting the point of no return, inevitably, a trip will open in whatever area I had just dropped off, making me wish I stopped for that ten-minute coffee break after all. Hindsight is a powerful and useless tool.

Today, things felt different. Within a minute after dropping off, a fresh call popped in nearby Harmarville, the next exit off Route 28. The trip was at The Valley Motel, never one to be confused with The Ritz-Carlton. Five minutes later, a gentleman and I were enroute to a Penn Hills address several miles away. He requested this to be a round trip, as he needed to "pick up something really quick from his cousin's crib," then return to the motel. I know I am at times skeptical, maybe it was a hunch, or perhaps those decades of study at cab-college raised a bright red flag to wave in my mind upon hearing the words round and trip together. I concluded that we were doing a drug run.

Whatever took place, we soon were on our way back to The Valley, another effortless $40 coming my way as we pulled into the parking lot of the humble hotel. Routine pleasantries were exchanged, and I was on my merry way.

As I resumed my trek on Route 28 towards the 'burgh, there was still faint hope for that elusive airport trip. Saturdays are typically slow travel days. Most people leaving for a weekend getaway are long gone by Friday night, with little incentive to return till Sunday night or Monday morning. Nevertheless, planes arrive and depart daily, even on Saturdays, so there is always that chance.

As I approached the 40th Street Bridge, several trips populated the screen in Bloomfield, Oakland, and Shadyside, calls I usually jump on without hesitation. As I pondered my next move, Zone 302, an offer I often resist, also appeared. My instinct said to hit that 302. The order was in the Sugar Top section of the Hill District, an area not known for frequent flyers. But hey, what a good day— Clarissa Street was bound for the Promised Land!

An elegant, well-spoken young lady from Ghana, my passenger was a graduate student at Pitt. Her command of English was superb compared to many of the students I encounter who were born in this country; there were no *likes* or *fer-sures* peppering her sentences. She spoke of how much she enjoyed studying and interning in our great city, and I loved hearing of her high hopes to permanently settle here. And the best part was that I now had a trifecta of consecutive $40 rides, this one rolling to $44, including the modest tip on her credit card.

Something I truly cherish about this fascinating profession are those brief interactions, the mini relationships that form during simple cab rides. Even the less than pleasant experiences, of which there have been far too many to count, are valued for the impact they have and the lessons they teach. However, I quickly forget 95% of the people with whom I cross paths, no matter how enlightening, entertaining, disdainful, or obnoxious they were.

The odd thing, which I feel to be more akin to me than to taxi drivers in general, is that I maintain a much more defined sense of place than of people. To this day, I still remember exact addresses and details of random trips from decades ago. In some cases, I can remember which specific cab number I was assigned that day. If I could jump into a time machine and set the year to, say, 1970, I could deliver my newspaper routes error free. Yet, while I can still recall the where and when and even some of the conversations from these three aforementioned trips, I'd be hard pressed to recognize the couple I took to the mall, the young man on his "business trip" from the motel, or the lovely lady from Ghana, one week afterwards.

On Saturday afternoon, the airport is a crapshoot at best. I joined a modest crowd of twenty-some taxis in the holding lot. I grazed on some offerings from my black vinyl lunch bucket, while exercising my mildly functioning brain with select readings from *The Pittsburgh Post-Gazette* to ease the wait. Within an hour, I was already among the front- four at the airport's taxi stand. The good day persevered.

The terminal seemed dead. I stood around, leaned against the cab, paced, rinsed, and repeated for a twenty-minute eternity as the three cabs ahead slowly received trips from luggage dragging stragglers. Finally, I was first up. As much as I thirst for trips to the airport, once there, all that I want in the world is to leave, with someone else's ass in close contact with my back seat and the meter ticking rapidly. Several more minutes crawled by without a soul in sight. At last, a bespectacled, middle- aged man walked my way. More caution flags—no luggage!

Not having bags at an airport is not necessarily a bad thing. I remember too well how airlines famously mishandle luggage from my side gig delivering those lost treasures during a previous sabbatical from cab life. The luggage-less client could be on a long layover or delay between flights, seeking to kill time at a local bar, restaurant, or even the Sunoco Station on the edge of the airport property. The gentleman approached as I awaited my mini fate. "Hello, would you go to Beaver Falls?"

"Sure!" I enthusiastically replied, my fears of a short one alleviated.

A small rust belt city whose glory days were a fading story, Beaver Falls was a decent trip, less than a thirty-mile straight shot northwest on the Beaver Valley Expressway. It should easily pay out at least $70 and allow a quick return to the airport holding lot. The positive karma continued.

The man chose to ride shotgun, which was fine with me. He was dressed casually, yet conservatively, clarifying as we pulled away from the curb that he wanted to do a round trip. A round trip to a depressed, drug- infested town? Not this again… dollar signs quickly eradicated my doubts. Jackpot!

He introduced himself as Carl, Dr. Carl Werts, a dentist from Glendale, California. He had been in the area attending a conference at Clarion State University, studying pioneering techniques in oral surgery. Naturally, I wished he were heading on the 100 mile plus trip to Clarion, PA instead of Beaver Falls. Several weeks earlier, I lucked into a $350 cab voucher from a local hospital to Clarion. I snapped out of my express fantasy cab trip and rejoined the current one.

Carl had just returned from Clarion, with several hours to kill before his westbound flight home. He decided to take a side trip to Beaver Falls, the Ohio River Valley town of his familial roots. It was a bucket list checkoff, searching for a sense of the place his father's extended family proclaimed as home, the place where they were from. This day was getting better and better for me. A round trip, devoid of pharmaceutical transactions, I was all in! This could even become *ancestry. com* in a cab.

I have always committed to being an exceptional ambassador for the Pittsburgh region, a natural born tour guide. Some of my favorite fares over the years were those of passengers requesting tours of all or specific parts of our region. However, as far as Beaver Falls was concerned, I knew jackshit. I knew how to get there. The layout of the town with its main drag and numbered streets did not require a genius to decipher. I recalled that a couple of famous people were born there, not that I could remember who they were in the moment. But I was up for the adventure and off we were to Beaver Falls. One of the first things to come into view upon entering town was a prominent, well-kept sign: *Beaver Falls – Hometown of Hall of Famer Joe Namath.* Oh yeah, *that* famous person, I should know that!

Our first order of business was achieved as we parked, allowing Carl to snap several pictures of the sign. Carl discussed how his father frequently recollected the famous Jets quarterback was indeed from his hometown. Just then, a flashback of a similar sign elsewhere came to mind. About ten years earlier, my son rode along with me on a baggage delivery run. Upon entering Langeloth, a small mining hamlet near the Pennsylvania- West Virginia border, we were treated to a similar sign, declaring: *Langeloth- Hometown of Barry Alvarez.* Neither Justin nor I had any idea who he was. The name rang a bell, yet I could only draw a blank. We even asked the lady at the house receiving the luggage; she had never even heard of him. The next day, with guidance from Google, we discovered that Barry was the legendary coach of the Wisconsin Badgers.

Back to Beaver Falls. Fortunately, Carl had contacted a cousin who knew the specifics of many locations where he could seek out his roots. As we wound our way through town, Carl seemed simultaneously surprised and disappointed by its appearance. He was unaware of the degree of economic decline of a place he last visited decades earlier. He recalled a bustling, homey, Mayberry-like town, a tree-lined main street dotted with prospering small businesses.

Instead, he witnessed boarded up windows under faded signs on dilapidated buildings along what used to be the city's thriving heart.

Carl briefed me on some of his family ties and connections. His grandfather, Henry Werts was a respected local dentist whose office integrated with the family home. What a shame those homelike medical and dental practices are so seldom seen in this modern world.

An early highlight of our tour was discovering the old Catholic Church his ancestors attended, likely a focal point in their lives. Carl appeared let down, but not shocked to see the building in disrepair, protected by an uneven, easily scalable chain link fence graced with a discolored metal *No Trespassing* sign. The towering steeple atop the building remained, maintaining a spiritual watch over the struggling town. While Carl paused, reflecting on Sunday morning traditions his ancestors enjoyed in better times, I lamely wondered how long ago the valuables and copper piping disappeared from inside of what was once a local center of worship and unity.

At the next stop, not far from the church, we pinpointed the home of Silas Werts, his great-grandfather and family patriarch. The house, a well-worn structure with weathered paint and smoke scars, reflected much of the surrounding city. As Carl continued his camera work, it was heartwarming to discover the house remained a home as a young couple came outside wondering why this old dude was stalking their property. Once Carl explained how his great-grandfather had called the same structure home at the turn of the previous century, they became willing allies in Carl's ancestry quest.

Several blocks away, we found his grandfather's former home and dental office. A two and a half story brick and siding home, this property was well preserved, as were most of the surrounding properties. As battle-scarred as Beaver Falls was, we managed to uncover several bright spots—the city still had great hope!

Our final stop was the cemetery, where Carl's ancestors rested in peace. We had good directions to the place, situated high atop a hillside at the city's eastern edge, offering scenic views of the valley below. Beaver Falls sprung to life; at least from this angle.

I find exploring cemeteries captivating, combining their serene environment and historical significance. While it was never my habit to hang out in graveyards, when situations put me in one, I often browse the headstones, imagining the lives these people may have lived. This cemetery was rather large, with an intriguing blend of older and newer burial sites.

The stone honoring Silas, Carl's great-grandfather, was also engraved with the name of his younger siblings, Peter, and Gertrude. Silas had lived from 1844-1921, 77 years, a decent lifespan for any era. I found it strange that Peter and Gertrude's birth years were listed as 1889 and 1883, respectively. As a rule, it is rare to find siblings with 40 to 45-year age differences, but who was I to question. My best guess was that Carl's great-grandmother may have died young and Silas remarried years later to a much younger wife. Or maybe the faded, barely readable 1844 inscription was originally meant to read 1874 or 1884? It was noteworthy that the dates of deaths of all three were close together: Peter in 1916, Silas in

1921 and Gertrude in 1922. Peter made it to a lifespan of a mere 27 years, while Gertrude lived to the ripe old age of 39.

We resumed our trek until coming upon our final piece of this wonderful puzzle. Fairly close to the cemetery's inner roadway in an older section of burial grounds, a trio of small, frayed stones stood together, the left one slanted away at an awkward angle. The surrounding weed plagued landscape seemed less attended to compared with other nearby plots. These were the resting places of Carl's father's siblings, who never had a chance to live long enough for Carl to call aunt or uncle. The tilted stone was Bertrand's, born in July of 1910, only to survive one week. The stone in the middle commemorated the short life of Elizabeth, who was granted just one day of life in February 1914. On the right rested Donald, who had lived long enough to at least earn the nickname, *Donnie*. Donnie only survived from January 1918 until February 1919, barely over a year. Spanish flu? I wondered what happened to these children, how cruel could life have been? I tried to imagine how long it had been since anyone visited these gravestones or remembered three abbreviated lives. I wished I had some flowers to offer, maybe even three small rocks to place upon these headstones, a timeless Jewish tradition of remembrance. A better me would have looked around and found something, but instead I stood quietly with hands in my pockets and a slight head bow.

Carl was ready to return to the airport, our adventure complete. He seemed content to have connected with his ancestral history, something I hoped would stay with him for the rest of his life. Speeding towards The Promised Land, we passed exit signs flashing names of similar river towns— *Industry... Midland... Shippingport... Aliquippa.* Surely within these places, countless biographies like those of the Beaver Falls' Werts family patiently awaited their turns to be heard. After delivering Carl safely back to the airport, I was handed two hundred- dollar bills and a sincere thank you for the adventure. I promised to share this story, as it was rewarding for me as well; far beyond the $200.

I returned to the lot, scavenging my lunch bucket remnants, thinking how good this day had been. A terrific one for me... then the light bulb flickered. I recalled those three weathered graves. Elizabeth was granted only a single day, a century ago. It was likely not a good day at all. How lucky we all are for every single day. Even when life sucks.

CHAPTER 37

Tipping Point

September 2014

The dawn of a beautiful weekend in the 'burgh. While "normal people" dot their i's and cross their t's for barbecues, nights-on-the-town, and getaways, I thoroughly vacuum cab #160 in preparation for my usual adventure as a weekend warrior.

Having finished my work week of puzzling bus drivers and scheduled service together for our local transit authority, I prepare for my weekend ritual dance with the canary-yellow, money-making 2010 Taurus. I dedicate a good twenty minutes to ensuring the taxi is sparkling clean inside and out, expecting to spend the equivalent of another full work-week with the cab. The passengers I transport (usually) deserve and (sometimes) appreciate my exceptionally clean cab. Even though the odometer reads north of 190,000 miles, people often mistake it for a new car. After exiting Yellow's antiquated car wash, I pull alongside my personal vehicle, a hand-me-down 2002 Honda minivan (I always get my wife's leftovers, *thanks Honey!*), and transfer my "cab-stuff," cleaning supplies and maps—I hate GPS— into the taxi's trunk. I am parked on Pennsylvania Ave, a block away from Yellow Cab's Manchester garage. This Pennsylvania Avenue offers nothing resembling The White House, but I managed to find a space near the strip club. If my Honda's headlights could magically transform into eyes over the weekend, it would never be bored.

The final touch of my taxi-prep ritual involves a generous spraying of *Fabreeze-Extra Strength* on the seats and carpets. The air freshener is my final prayer for a clean start to the weekend. I thoroughly embrace the theory that this extra work will pay off big time in the tip department. The truth? At times it does. Most often, it makes little difference.

Diverting from my Friday routine of heading towards Oakland, the city's bustling university hub, today I ice-break Downtown. Yes, there is strategy involved; a big convention is breaking up, there will be plenty of airports to go around. My goal, like many other drivers, is to lead off my day with a homerun, a trip to the airport. Crawling through rush hour traffic, I head for The Omni William Penn, a source of thousands, perhaps millions, of voyages to The Promised Land throughout its distinguished history.

As I impatiently inch through William Penn Way traffic, I observe someone approaching the hotel's taxi stand where two cabs await. When parked on a cab stand, it is protocol to accept whatever trip may come your way. The customer, a middle -aged woman wearing librarianesque glasses, toting a small Macy's shopping bag, is abruptly turned away by the first taxi—not a yellow one, by the way— and he drives away from the cabstand, empty handed. The woman approaches the next taxi, a yellow one. Following a brief exchange with that driver, I watch as he too refuses her trip, pulling off the stand, his left hand flailing out the window, pointing at the other departing cab and shaking his head. The lady is left stranded, purse and bag in hand, still without a ride.

Well, I guess she ain't goin' to the port! I deduce, my pseudo analytical skillset shining. Yes, I am seeking an airport trip, but she is going *somewhere*, she still needs a cab. Moment of truth—the green light! Should I divert left, hang a last second right... I decide to stay the course, straight to the hotel's now vacated taxi stand.

Pulling to the curb, I motion for the lady to hop in. She instead approaches my open window, apologetically asking if I would mind going to Mt. Lebanon, a well to-do nearby suburb in Pittsburgh's South Hills. The reality, in my world, is this; at rush hour, the last thing I hope for is a trip to Mt Lebanon. There is no quick way there, especially in traffic at this time of day. Plus, everything else about this situation points to disaster. A conservative looking, middle-aged female, justifiably dissatisfied with poor service, going to Mt Lebanon, an area known for high income and subpar tips. Plus, this could shatter my dreams of a trip to The Promised Land!

"Sure, Miss, wherever you need to go." I manage a sincere tone.

"Oh, thank you, thank you!" She gets in and we're on the way.

I wonder, why is *she* thanking *me*? She needs a cab, and the last time I checked, I was driving one. After establishing the specifics of her destination, I decided to ask what the deal was with the other two cabs.

She said she was turned away by four different drivers before I had stopped. This totally sucks! Pittsburgh's taxi services are, perhaps deservingly, getting much negative press as controversial new competition in the form of smartphone taxi impersonators like Lyft and Uber make their imprints.

I apologize for the bad business practices of my peers, assuring her that most cab drivers are not that way, while quietly assuring myself that a little white lie here and there never hurt anyone.

"Well, I understand and I'm really not that upset," she replies. "Besides, *they* missed out because I happen to be a *very* good tipper."

Oh no! The king of red flags! Those who proclaim themselves to be great tippers often wind up being the opposite. Now, this is the perfect storm. Conservative, middle-aged female, going to an area known for mediocre tips telling me how good a tipper she is; I am up Shit's Creek! However, I maintain my composure, keeping my happy face. And no matter the situation, or my overthought theories, she was a sincerely nice lady.

"I appreciate that— I'm just glad to be able to give you a ride." I feel almost like I really meant that. The rest of the ride remains pleasant. She was visiting her elderly mother, who lived in Mt Lebanon. And, for a Friday, the traffic was nowhere near as horrifying as I projected.

Her destination is a medium-rise apartment building on Washington Road, the borough's main drag. I stop the meter as we pulled in front of the building, the total fare reading $14.70.

"Thank you so much! Here, the rest is for you." She hands over two folded bills.

Oh no, folded money! People often fold their bills to conceal cheapness at tipping time. This could not possibly be a ten and a five, could it? She was very nice; probably two tens, a five-buck tip. Decent, though not incredible. But I would be pleased with that—33%!

I had not yet looked at the money. "Well, thank you Miss, enjoy your..." There were *two twenties*— 40 BUCKS! "Uh—hey, do you need any change?"

"No, that's yours. I did say that I have always been a good tipper."

"Wow, well, thank you! And here's my number if you ever need a ride anywhere." I awkwardly scribble my name and cell number on the back of a blank receipt.

"Thank you, I will certainly keep this. I don't use cabs often, but I'll put you in my phone. Have a great weekend." She strolls toward the building, turning, and waving as she disappears into its entrance.

Merging into the Washington Road traffic, I happily pocket my $25 tip. Someday, I may attempt to write a thesis entitled *The Psychology of Tipping*. For now, I genuinely appreciate people, like this lady, who value and acknowledge good customer service. I also thank the taxi-gods for the anonymous cabbies who left her high and dry at the William Penn.

I promptly headed back downtown. As I cruise Grant Street, Pittsburgh's grand corridor of commerce, law, and big buildings, within minutes, two designer suits carrying fine leather briefcases offer a confident New York cab hail. I swiftly shift to the curb lane.

"Airport!"

I just love karma—especially the good kind.

CHAPTER 38

Jitneys for White People

October 2014

Taxicabs have shared a grumbling coexistence with illegal jitneys forever. This relationship was tolerable by cabbies, as most jitney trips originated in poor and minority neighborhoods, where few cabs cared to venture. Jitney drivers trolled urban supermarkets, scooping up fares cab drivers did not mind avoiding. Pittsburgh's cabbies preferred loading their trunks with Promised Land bound baggage, as opposed to shopping bags stuffed with groceries, topped with bundles of collard greens and kale destined for humble abodes in nearby 'hoods. While this uneasy and unspoken cooperation between the licensed, marked cabs and unregulated, illegal jitneys persevered, there were territorial conflicts. Adventurous jitneys competed with taxis at the Amtrak, Greyhound, and Megabus terminals. They parked nearby, soliciting inside the stations' entrances, hustling trips by posing as taxis to naïve travelers while miming a steering motion to those who seemed familiar. Public Utility Commission regulations prohibited taxicab drivers from such solicitation; they could only watch helplessly as the jitneys whisked away business.

During the past decade, jitney culture became even bolder. Sporting fake rooftop taxi marquees affixed to vehicles advertising *AVAILABLE, SHUTTLE, CAR SERVICE, RIDE,* or, even more ballsy, *TAXI,* they unabashedly paraded through the South Side and stalked other evening hotspots. Unsuspecting, too drunk to care clientele gravitated towards the jitneys, happy to have a ride. Jitneys often charged significantly higher rates than taxi fare, leaving the riders with the impression of being ripped off by unscrupulous cab drivers.

Whether perception, reality, or somewhere in between, jitneys thrived because of a deserved perception of inadequate taxi and public transit service. While it is unfair to expect hundreds of smiling taxi operators to magically appear out of nowhere every Saturday at exactly 2 AM, it is reasonable to conclude that Pittsburgh's cab companies have done a less than stellar job serving the community in recent years. Yellow Cab had developed a dubious reputation, one which no sensible business would want to advertise, paving the way for the competition to mercilessly eat away its market share.

Smaller cab companies, limos, and car services emerged, most following the proper licensing and regulating protocol. Few blended into the market with success, others held their own while the rest failed and faded away. All these competitors combined would never have a fraction of the market impact of Lyft and Uber. As each conglomerate deploys similar business models, we will reference Uber as an umbrella term for both platforms.

Upon entering the local marketplace, Uber's business strategies for Pittsburgh were unremarkably similar with their modes of operations in peer cities. While taxi and limousine companies needed to take great care to jump through appropriate hoops, dot the proper i's and cross the right t's, Uber deemed itself to be above anyone's local rules. They announced their presence as not a transportation, but a tech company, and rationalized having no obligation to follow state or local laws regarding background checks, insurance, age and condition of vehicles, rates, or anything else. Like their launches in similar markets, Uber legitimized itself to the populace by enlisting a high-profile celebrity to, by sheer happenstance, be their first customer. In our situation, who was better than a beloved Pittsburgh Steelers defensive lineman? And the cherry on top was an advertising campaign proclaiming themselves as a superior taxi service while simultaneously asserting *not* to be a taxi service!

Unwittingly and dimwittedly, local media and political leaders fell in love with Uber, sanctioning the illegal jitney operation, albeit with a wink and nod. This was a new reality to face, an uncertain, uncomfortable world.

The first groups to gravitate away from cabs and towards Uber were hipsters, Millennials, and techies. Instead of calling, or even using an app to order a taxi, Uber became the new way to go to the next place to be. Taxis were suddenly uncool. Business began a rapid decline; call it a tailspin. The times were changing; not for the better.

In the beginning, Uber concentrated their campaign in the middle and upper- class neighborhoods in the East End, attracting mostly young professionals and college students.

While traditional jitneys focused on lower income areas like The Hill District, Homewood, or Mount Oliver, where cab service was marginal, Uber targeted well- to- do communities like Shadyside, Highland Park, and Squirrel Hill, where taxis were always easily attainable.

And it worked! What could be more fulfilling for an up-and-coming techie-hipster than pressing a button on the latest iPhone summoning a car to Whole Foods to transport him and his reusable canvas grocery bags peeking with quinoa, baguettes, and certified organic baby kale to his Shadyside loft? What—privilege! Jitneys for white people were here to stay.

Uber kale.

Uber or Taxi?

CHAPTER 39

Extinction

May 2015

Following intensive car vacuum therapy and a shower in the company car wash, aging cab number 160 is primed to conquer the world. Or at least the 'burgh. I head to Oakland, filling up at the Marathon station on Forbes Avenue. With a clean cab and full tank, I am ready for my own weekend marathon.

I pull alongside the gas station on McKee Place by a *No Parking Anytime* sign, which has served as a de facto cab stand for decades. Across the street stands the Hilton Garden Inn, a busy hotel in the hub of this concentrated center of education, medicine, and technology.

I book into dispatch zone #305 and note my position as the fifth cab in the queue for the area. There are scant few pending fares, none nearby, or appearing to be worth a chase. I merely seek any icebreaker to begin my shift. People sometimes walk over to the cab stand, or the hotel's doorman will motion or whistle for a guest, although nowhere near as often as they used to.

So, I sit. And sit some more, intermittently starting the engine, firing up the AC, glancing at the hotel. Twenty minutes pass and I've only progressed one spot in the dispatch queue, to number four. A man wearing a business suit exits the hotel, toting luggage. Airport?! He stares intently at his phone, ignoring my presence. I am tempted to roll down the window and ask if he needs a cab, but either pride, or the probability of the answer of an affirmative no stops me. Five minutes later, a red Prius rolls up, rewarding the man with positive reinforcement from his app-tap.

"Uber-motherfucker!" I holler, only loud enough to echo within my cab's confines, unclear if it's the Uber driver, his passenger, a changing world, or myself I am angry with.

The frustration persists. Twenty more minutes crawl by. My patience dwindles. Three scantily attired young women, probably Pitt students, congregate ten feet in front of my cab. Typifying their generation, their smartphones captivate them. The blaring horn of a bus intercepts my thoughts, as a car cuts it off diagonally, coming to an abrupt halt in the middle of the intersection—no blinkers, no turn -signals— a near miss! The clueless trio look away from their devices and saunter towards the traffic disrupting Uber. Why didn't they take this cab? I was right there!

More time passes, it's been over an hour. At last, the MDT buzzes, *Fare Waiting*; this torture finally ends. The pick-up is at Carnegie Museum of Natural History, a young couple from Seattle in town for a wedding, returning to their downtown hotel. They enjoyed our museums and were especially impressed with our dinosaur collection. I steer my passengers to lead the direction of the conversation.

They did not mention the weather, nor ask for recommendations to spend their leisure time in Pittsburgh. They did not inquire about dining options. They did not even want to know what time my shift started, or how many eons I've been doing this dreadful job. They did not even want to hear a crazy cab story!

"So," the lady inquires, "how much is Uber affecting your business?"

My half-truth of a reply is that Uber has a minor, but noticeable impact. What I really want is to scream *Uber-mother fuckers!* from the top of my lungs, but somehow manage to refrain. The truth is I now feel obsolete. Extinct. Like those other dinosaurs.

CHAPTER 40

Imaginary Stars

January 2016

Dearest Reader:

Recently, a message appeared on my Android phone, congratulating me on completing my 500ᵗʰ Uber trip. I can imagine what you must think. *Hypocrite! WTF? Traitor! After all these years, all those cab stories, all this anti- Uber ranting, you sold out to the enemy. You suck!*

You're right; I caved. Truth is, I have been *"driving with Uber"* (what Uncle Uber likes to call it) for several months, albeit on a very limited basis. I continue clinging to my status with the cab company but with decreasing frequency. I refuse to break up with my faithful flip phone, reserving the "smartphone" – not my term—for Uber, partly because I'm technically challenged, also to detach from Planet Uber when not *ubering*. And, yes, I do abhor how Uber has evolved into a noun, verb, adjective, and adverb.

When I decided to write this book, it was with the sincerest intent to allow you to view the world through the unique lens of a taxi driver. Uber was not a remote dot on the radar screen. And it certainly was *not a bad trip* until Uber's avalanche of disruption. Not so long ago, to disrupt was rude. Suddenly, disruption became the most admired practice in the business world. Uber's disruption and destruction of the business I knew and loved was bad enough, but I had my own message for them— *Thanks for disrupting my book writing process, Uncle Uber!*

Prior to caving in, to comprehend my culture shock, I joined a variety of social media rideshare drivers' groups, rarely posting or offering input. My objective was to understand the attraction of drivers and passengers to these so-called rideshare companies, which at that point operated as unlicensed jitneys. I never conveyed whether I was an Uber driver, Lyft driver, taxi driver, curious observer, or conscientious objector, and my credentials as part of the "rideshare community" went unchallenged.

My initial impression of Uber's invasion brought one word to mind – cult. The Gen X and Millennial cab riders flocked to Uber like mindless sheep. Uber advertised rates competitive with local taxi fare while strategically marketing free rides and discounted codes online. The cab company's reaction? They shrugged and did nothing.

The demand for Ubers often exceeded the supply of available drivers, triggering frequent and heavy surge pricing. Although surge fares were ridiculously higher than taxis, affluent young professionals and Mommy's credit card toting students did not mind at all. This had overnight become *the* coolest and most convenient way to get around. They now could wave their proverbial middle fingers at the increasingly idled yellow taxis. And I dare not omit the foremost important sociological factor in the whole equation—their phones *told* them to do it!

For drivers, Uber offered a delicious, tempting lure of a longer-term bait and switch strategy. There were few local drivers at first, coupled with an unlimited volume of business. Those who got in on the ground floor raked in excellent money, running surge after surge fare.

So, what's cultish about that? Many of the drivers, especially the younger ones, were mesmerized with Uncle Uber, drinking gallon upon gallon of whatever Kool-Aid du jour was on the menu. I suppose it beat the fuck out of working as a Starbuck's barista! Yet, more than a few people abandoned decent, career-track types of jobs, financing expensive, new vehicles to join the parade, becoming full-fledged phone-drones.

Common themes dominated Uber social media world. There was a genuine disdain for cab drivers and hatred towards the taxi industry. Cabs were dirty, disgusting, they smelled bad. Cab drivers were rude, they never showed up, they couldn't speak English—wow! The Uber drivers, on the other hand, were a collective breath of fragrant air. They were cool. Hip. Super-smart people driving awesome cars. Downright special! For some strange reason, inhabitants of Uber-land had this unique knowledge that cabbies were union members. This had not been the case in Pittsburgh since 1984. Anti-union rhetoric polluted the threads, as these ultra-intellectuals envisioned themselves as sophisticated entrepreneurs, upwardly mobile—well, they were mobile—pillars of an imaginary business community. I proudly maintained my standing as a smelly scumbag in a dirty cab.

Then, there was heroism. Uber drivers embraced this grand illusion of themselves as dauntless. Staying out late on weekend nights ferrying drunks across bridges for double and triple the standard taxi fare were anointed selfless acts of noble community service. Uber drivers were convinced they saved hundreds of lives every weekend, eliminating the countless tragedies which would have resulted from hordes of drunk drivers. Gee, thanks guys!

Absorbing this bullshit became too much, so I emerged from underneath my troll bridge. I did not want to burst bubbles or fracture fragile egos, but the lifesaver delusions were beyond absurd. I *kind of politely* pointed out how taxis, car services, designated drivers, and buses filled that niche amicably for years. I would be rich had I saved a dollar for each instance I transported drunks from point A to point B before Uber existed. Firefighters, police officers, nurses, doctors, military personnel, medical responders—those are the heroes! Uber drivers, cabbies—are you kidding? Get over yourselves!

Another annoying aspect of Uber World was the overuse of buzzwords and euphemisms. Drivers are not drivers; they are *partners*. Really? I questioned my online Uber buddies if they ever attended a partners' meeting. One, to his credit, who was looking for a way out, posted his resume, listing this career heading in his work experience section: *Partnership in Uber*. Call me a skeptic who is baffled how a grown adult who logs into an app to do incremental driving gigs, where he or she has no authority on pricing, or policy, and could be deactivated at any time for any reason or no reason, believes he or she is a key player in a business partnership.

Next, we have *community*. Not as illogical as partner, but, come on. What community is this…a community of partners? We are told of *Community Guidelines*. What are those? Maybe because partners are independent contractors, and not employees, there are guidelines to follow instead of actual rules. I'm puzzled… does Uncle Uber provide a business partnership? Is it community service? Or, if liability issues arise, is it magically *just an app*, nothing to see here?

There is an allotted parking area for rideshare drivers at the airport, akin to the taxi holding lot. When I get an Uber airport trip, I sometimes take a walk for exercise, or stroll to the nearby Sunoco for a bathroom break. Uber provides us valued partners with the gift of three indescribably disgusting Port-A-Johns, which I have neither the courage nor stomach to utilize. Random social interactions of small groups break out in the parking area, none of which could pass as a community activity or partners meeting.

The most bizarre behavior in rideshare culture are drivers posting screenshots of their pay and star ratings. Has anyone inhabiting a normal work environment ever shared pictures of their paystubs on social media? It reminds me of little kids showing off their report cards after school. Does it provide psychological reinforcement that their partnerships are working out? The most baffling to me are when drivers share screenshots boasting of "long trips."

Long rides in cabs are fantastic, paying excellent money. In an Uber, not so much. Taxis, being regulated, have always operated within defined geographically bound areas. Fares going beyond those boundaries are compensated for the dead miles on the trip back. Some companies charge the meter amount plus half, others apply surcharges. Yellow's meters double the mileage charge after a given distance. Once the trip passes the twenty- mile mark, the metered per mile fare automatically multiplies.

One common trip posted in local Uber chats is the trip from The Promised Land to Morgantown, home of West Virginia University. My most recent taxi trip there was worth a healthy $264 on a credit card, including a $10 tip. Great trip! Minus the 4% credit card fee the cab company charges to process, I realized a gross profit of approximately $253. Nice!

Uber's trip? A recent one paid the driver $73, meaning the passenger paid well north of $100 for the trip, including airport and safe-ride fees pocketed by Uber. Yes—there is really a surcharge for *trust* and *safety!* This is an approximate eighty- mile trip each way. Our Uber buddy seemed quite enchanted with his payout, but the reality is he eventually needed to return home. The chance of a return trip is somewhere between slim and none. The I.R.S. allowance of 55 cents per mile is a breakeven point for expenses when using a vehicle for business purposes. If there is validity to that number, the $73 he thinks he "made" costs over $90 to run. Not economically viable. However, Uber drivers around the country guzzle this peculiar flavor of long- lasting Kool-Aid.

And, finally, there are stars. Those imaginary sparkling, gold stars. Uncle Uber and his ilk convinced the world that Uber is a universal five-star experience. Star ratings are nothing new. Hotels, movies, restaurants, resorts, and some things outside the scope of our imaginations are graded respectively between one and five stars. Some even upgrade to diamonds!

In the real world, which Uber seldom inhabits, few businesses achieve the highly coveted five-star rating. I do not know the exact statistics but am confident that less than one percent of hotels or restaurants consistently earn such accolades. Some, but nowhere near a majority, earn four-star ratings, signifying excellence in quality and service.

Uber gods program their worshipers to assume five-star ratings as a starting point, rather than an earned accomplishment. On a scale of one to five, the median is a three. If the service is acceptable, yet not exceptional, three stars would be a common rating. Two stars, mediocre, perhaps lacking attention to detail. A one star—not so good. Any service provider rated one star needs to reevaluate their practices if they wish to survive. Four stars, once again, excellent. But five stars have always signified the top of the ladder, exemplary, the finest—the best of the best.

Stays at hotels such as Four Seasons or the Ritz-Carlton, where details are meticulously attended to, where staff exceed expectations to please their guests, are expected to be five-star experiences. After all, the guests pay for and anticipate five- star service. In our city, there are some fine four-star hotels, yet none are currently rated at five stars.

Kate's flight touches down on a Sunday evening. Her company secured a room at the Pittsburgh Fairmont, one of our premium four-star establishments. Kate is pleased her employer awarded her such fine accommodations for her business trip.

Kate wheels her luggage to door number four at the airport, opening her Uber app for a ride downtown. She notices four taxis lingering at the cabstand yet opts to join a growing crowd of waiting phone drones. Her app-tap instantly connects her with Kyle and his Toyota Corolla. Kyle, meanwhile, is finishing the remnants of his Chorizo taco as Uncle Uber pings to pick up awaiting Kate, sporting an impressive 4.88 rating at door #4.

Kate is somewhat concerned with Kyle's 4.71 rating, and was hoping for a nicer car, like the Mercedes she snagged on her earlier ride. But she decides to grin and bear it, as she cannot wait to get to her four-star (not 4.71, but 4.00) hotel for a hot bath.

Kyle pulls up, Kate hops in back. Not much leg room, but hey, it's an Uber. Although the car reeks of refried beans, Kyle is polite, attempting the usual dead- end small talk customary to such encounters. Kyle safely and efficiently transports Kate to her destination. As she thanks Kyle for the ride, Kate swipes five stars on her *very* smart phone as she hands the doorman a crisp five- dollar bill for opening the door of the Corolla. Kyle, naively thrilled with his $17.96 payout, reciprocates with five stars Kate's way. Kyle will remember Kate as the lady who could afford a $400 hotel and tip the doorman but not the Uber driver than for any of the content of their conversation during the ride. Kate will remember her ride in the eight-year- old Corolla with Kyle as *fine*, despite the lingering Chorizo odor on her coat. Yet, in this strange new world of Uber, they robotically rate each other the obligatory perfect five because this is the way Uncle Uber said it should be.

Why all these stars? Will they help the Uber driver pay his rent or mortgage? Or are they really a psychological control mechanism? Both partner and client believe that because they are so highly regarded by their incredible ratings of *almost* five golden stars. They will surely keep coming back.

Don't believe me? Just check your smartphone. It will never steer you wrong.

Sincerely,

Howie—Your Uber Driver

Uber logo, reverse Pac-Man, or commercial-grade toilet paper?

Imaginary star rating.

Door number 4, where Kate meets Kyle.

Begging for stars.

CHAPTER 41

Wet Paint

June 2016

The semi-intelligent dashboard mounted device instructs me to meet Jeffrey at 649 Penn Avenue. My inner cabby instantly recognizes the address as *Meat and Potatoes*, an acclaimed player in Pittsburgh's growing reputation as a foodie's paradise.

A well-attired couple, a tall fiftyish man with brown presidential hair and an alluring, dark- haired woman stand among a steady stream of black and gold clad passersby, gazing into their iPhones. I slow the unmistakably, blue Honda Civic mirroring the photo on their app to a halt. The man, after several seconds, notices the only blue Honda parked curbside with an Uber symbol inside its windshield and opens the back door. "Howard?"

"Jeffrey?" I state the obvious as his companion slides across the back seat. *Nice legs!*

I don't bother telling them to call me "Howie," or assume that Jeffrey prefers "Jeff." Jeffrey introduces his wife, Diana. They are up from Columbus, Ohio for a weekend getaway.

"So," Diana recites the inevitable, universal question, "how long have you been driving for Uber?" As much as the big picture changes, the more certain things remain the same.

"Oh, just for a few months," I reply, camouflaging my eye roll. Mundane, yet pleasant small talk continues for the duration of the brief ride to their hotel. As they depart, I wish them an enjoyable rest of the weekend and they well-wish me back. No tip. None is expected, as Uncle Uber informed the world—*there is no need to tip.*

Welcome to my less than brave new world. For the first time in decades, I miss hearing that *so how long have you been driving a taxi* line. Uber is for real; now even legal! It is not just a jitney service for privileged white people and tech happy Millennials. Everybody's ubering! Young people, old people, working people, lazy people, crazy people, rich people, poor people, Asian people, Brown people, Black people, people like Diana and Jeffrey, even teenage people. Incidentally, Uber's *Community Guidelines* stipulate no one under eighteen is permitted to ride without an adult. When did transportation for hire become an R-rated event? Yet, I frequently encounter obviously high school aged kids with Uber accounts. Should I card them? Perhaps hire a bouncer?

I remain semi-active with the cab company, rationing my spare time between taxi and Uber, my appearances at Yellow becoming less and less frequent. With the bills piling up, I increasingly accept overtime at my full-time Port Authority job, allocating less time for my side gigs. As much as I prefer being on the streets collecting money to meet fascinating people, the dispatcher overtime rate exceeding fifty bucks per hour is hard to ignore. While I still make halfway decent money on the cab, it is nowhere close to what once was, as Uber continues siphoning market share.

Well, why not forget the cab and only work Uber? The app is crazy busy, especially on weekends. At times, you drop one fare off to have another client waiting three doors down. I love that part! However, there is this minor issue — the money sucks.

Since invading this market, Uber has dropped its rates four times, to the ridiculous rate of 90 cents per mile—on par with cab fare—in 1980! After Uber takes their 25% cut, I find myself crawling in traffic for an astronomical 68 cents per mile. And this is only compounded by the *there is no need to tip culture* cemented by Uncle Uber.

When cabs were king, I would often turn down overtime at my real job. True, I seldom averaged $45 to $50 per hour driving a cab, but the money was exceptional for a second job. I could not ignore the adrenaline rush I felt each weekend as I jumped into my cab. It was who I was, a part of life I weirdly loved. Even though I often came home with an aching back and sore knees after double digit hours in the driver's seat, whining to my wife about douche- baggy passengers, how I should have done this instead of that, it was all okay. I loved the thrill of chasing down long trips, discovering another obscure corner of the city I swore I knew every inch of, or finding those golden needles in impossible haystacks. I cherished the not knowing who, where, or what to expect, if the next trip would be my last, whether I would live to see another shift.

The decline accelerated. Everywhere I turned, I observed car after car with Lyft and Uber decals adorning their windshields. It got to the point where I didn't even need to see the window sticker to spot Uber phone drones. When you see moving vehicles with their drivers hypnotized by lit-up, dash mounted phones, only occasionally glancing at the road, abruptly braking without flashers or signals, you are witnessing Uber in action. When car doors are carelessly flung into the left lane of passing or oncoming traffic, this is ridesharing protocol. Yes, I know what you're thinking; cabbies drive like assholes! And you're right. Cabbies are among the most aggressive drivers. However, most of *those* assholes remember to turn on their flashers, instruct their passengers to exit *stage right,* and at least *try* to stop in a safe and sensible spot.

By mid-summer, I was averaging only one or two shifts per month at Yellow, with a few hours of Uber sprinkled in. People were no longer taking cabs. There was more than enough blame to go around. Politicians, firmly in the pockets of Uber, did everything to create an unfair and uneven playing field. Yellow Cab enacted consistently bone-headed business decisions, like cutting the local dispatchers and operators, exporting the operation to a southern "right to work" state. To put it bluntly, these moves made the company's already dreadful reputation for service even worse. Farming out dispatch duties in an area with the complex topography and spaghetti-like street network of Pittsburgh to people with little knowledge of the city was never a good idea.

Yellow finally woke up and realized, *Pittsburgh, we have a problem!* In the spring, all the cab drivers were summoned in groups to mandatory meetings, acknowledging the fact that the taxi business had fallen into the toilet. The cab company did not exactly present it that way, but it was what it was. In these meetings, we learned that Yellow Cab, the iconic, undeniable, recognized industry leader, would soon become obsolete. All the cars would eventually be repainted one shade or another of an obscure silvery gray and rebranded along with a new- fangled ride app. Believe it or not, most major taxi firms embraced these apps for years before anyone ever muttered the word "uber."

In 2013, our taxis were decorated with trim and decals celebrating 100 years of serving the city. How many businesses have ever achieved the century mark? Will anybody, seriously, remember Uber in the year 2113? They could always Google it…wait —will anyone even remember Google?

Three years later, the geniuses at the helm came up with their grand idea. Paint over that legendary, familiar bright yellow, the color that always stood out in a sea of traffic, screaming "riders welcome!" Discard the traditional checkered trim, which for a century conveyed taxi legitimacy. Had the taxicab industry's reputation sunk so low that it no longer wished to be associated with itself?

For the final touch, that *Y word* on those little lit-up hats adorning the tops of taxis would be no more. I suppose it just wasn't right to designate a fleet of fifty shades of gray vehicles

"Yellow" anyhow. As the corporate logic dictated, that Y word would be replaced by using the next, and, ironically, the final letter in the alphabet —Z.

Thus, began the era of *Zee-Zee-Tripp.* *

*Not the actual name, but close enough.

FINAL CHAPTER

Stage Four

Fall 2016

*Z*ee-Zee-Tripp could not possibly paint their entire 300 plus fleet of cabs gray overnight. Any yellow paint lurking around the body shop was destined to rest in peace.

Over a year before the announced rebranding, the writing was on the wall. Each newly procured vehicle was simply decaled with Yellow Cab's trim, logos, and marquees, sans the yellow color. Black, white, green, red, and blue, joined by conveniently silver and gray cars, maintained their original paint despite their rebirth as "Yellow" cabs. Newer remaining yellow leftovers were transformed into silver or gray *Zee* cars, while the middle aged, yet too young for retirement cabs completed their life sentences in traditional yellow attire.

As the older cabs, especially the Crown-Vics, inched towards their final days, the company's fleet manager was granted carte blanche to modernize the fleet. Toyota was in the process of phasing out its entire Scion brand. To their credit, *Zee-Zee-Tripp* wisely acquired several dozen virgin XBs, the practical, boxy flagship of the Scion family. The incoming XBs were pre-adorned with the prescribed factory gray color, ready to be decaled with *Zee -trim* and pressed into action. Gently used Hyundai Santa Fe SUVs, along with Chrysler and Kia minivans in varying shades of silvery gray, also came to the party. To complete this automotive salad, a dozen preowned Priuses joined the *Zee- parade.* Rumors swirled that they were retired Uber lease cars from the west coast. I could not help but notice the remnants of halfway peeled off Uber stickers inside the windshields of some of the cars. Even during the end stages of life, you need to embrace its little ironies.

While all the gray stuff played out, I kept my foot in the door, making occasional guest appearances. To my amazement, the cage dispatchers were kind enough to keep my driver's number assigned on 160, my precious yellow Taurus. Still looking new and running well, the 319,000-number screaming from the odometer was the likely deal breaker in the decision to not convert it to *Zee-zee-gray.* I proudly continued driving my favorite yellow holdover into the battlefield.

For the past several years, I was one of a select few weekend warriors guaranteed a steady, premium cab. Like me, the senior cage dispatchers were relics of a bygone era. They knew I took pride in my work, the cab would be taken care of, and returned in one piece. Perhaps being a reliably generous tipper throughout the decades never hurt. But my increasing disinterest in coming to work with any degree of consistency inevitably caught up and 160 was reassigned. There was no reason to be upset about losing my steady, yellow companion, as my attendance became alarmingly unsteady.

When I did show up, they always managed to find me one of the newer Scions or Santa Fes. Despite resembling a box on wheels, the Scion was a peppy, fun car with a decent balance of cargo space and comfort. Santa Fe's were also terrific vehicles to work with. It was the first time in my prolonged cab career that the company incorporated SUVs into its fleet, the most versatile vehicles for taxi use since the Checker days.

I connected with Alex who was assigned to a weekly lease on one of the Santa Fes. He was seeking a partner to hold down the cab one or two weekends per month, allowing him a breather from taxi slavery. Realizing my days of cabbing every weekend were distant memories, this was the perfect arrangement. Age and health concerns signaled it was time to cut back the eighty- hour work weeks. Driving only when Alex needed a break worked well for both of us, even rejuvenating my enthusiasm for the cab business.

I continued ubering here and there, but never for a moment felt the same level of passion that I had from my time as a *real* cab driver. Regardless of the absolute domination of Uber and its rival cousins, I could still find my niche behind the wheel of a cab. Decades of experience, coupled with uncompromised knowledge of *my* city triumphed over any instructions from Uncle Uber's algorithms. Although the volume of taxi business which once existed was never coming back, I optimized from what little remained. The few fares filtering to cabs included greetings from passengers like *I couldn't get an Uber because my phone died,* or *Uber's surging ridiculously high,* but I just bit my tongue and graciously took the trips. Between accepting overtime from Port Authority, my infrequent, yet successful taxi weekends, and sparse hours of sprinkled -in phone-droning, I struck a satisfactory semblance of a work- life balance.

Well, maybe not. Like the good old days, I was again making decent money, including a jackpot exceeding $1200 over an October Steelers game weekend. It was due more to dumb luck, like stumbling into long trips and a $100 tipper, rather than some magical rebirth of the glory days of yellow under the gray banner of *Zees*. That luck ran its course, however, when Alex informed me the powers at *Zee-Zee-Tripp* threatened to relinquish his steady cab if he did not agree to keep it 24/7. I understood, no surprise.

I decided to try my luck the following Friday. The only available cabs were a beater eight- year-old Impala with 430,000 miles and a dirty Dodge van. Knowing beggars have few options, I strolled to the cab yard to ponder my choices. Both cars were blessed with an unholy trinity of musty odors, dried up food stains, and tobacco remnants. I returned to the cage, tossed in the keys, and said, "thanks, but no thanks." Chris and I enjoyed a nice Friday dinner out for a change. Saturday and Sunday, I swallowed my pride, stuck the Uber emblem in my Honda's windshield and made some money ping ponging around town.

Three more weekends came and went. Some overtime at my job, a busy Uber app, and more free time became effective painkillers for my taxi-less withdrawal. Often, when logging on with Uncle Uber, I was reminded of the irony of how closely their newest logo resembled a roll of toilet paper. Yes, it's a shitty business, but I was glad to have that roll in reserve.

The cab company's unwritten rule of showing once per month to remain in good standing still applied. A good month had passed since my previous lease. Part of me felt it was time to call it a day, perhaps a career. A bigger part of me could not just walk away.

To keep my iron in the *Zee-* fire, I needed to squeeze another shift under my belt. I had a scheduled vacation day for the Tuesday before Thanksgiving, traditionally a busy week for cabs. Many regulars take that week off, choosing to enjoy the holiday with friends and family—like normal people do. I usually drove at least part of Thanksgiving week, the heaviest travel period of the year.

I went down to *Zee-Zee-Tripp* that Monday after work. As I walked towards the garage along Beaver Avenue, I noticed the cab lot was somewhat full, yet not near to the degree as expected. Maybe some drivers who normally would forgo the holidays sacrificed an extra day or two to compensate for their decreased income sucked away by Uber. Nonetheless, it would be no trouble to secure a respectable vehicle for a 24-hour lease. I even spotted my old friend, 160, buried in the corner of the lot, unrecognizable, caked with dirt, fading into an unsightly, jaundiced hue.

The cashier offered cab #159, a dark gray Santa Fe, a twin of #259 cab I recently shared with Alex. It was clean, requiring only a quick vacuum. The price for a 24-hour lease was $128, which was fine in better times, but a steep nut to crack in this hostile business climate. Piece of cake, I thought. The plan was to work maybe five or six hours that night, then start early on Tuesday, and finish out the lease.

I logged on, eager to roll, but noticed there were too many cabs, way more than usual, scattered throughout the service area with virtually no business on the board. No problem. I've been doing this long enough to know how to separate the men from the boys. I was always most productive when business was slow to moderate; more proactive, aggressively chasing instead of overthinking, or cherry picking.

There is slow, but, then there is *s-l-o-w*. I worked a few hours, trying for any trip I could get, but with little success. It was beyond frustrating to follow a Greyhound and be the only cab at the station while a couple dozen people poured out, all scrambling for their Uber and Lyft blind dates. Not one person took a cab. I scrounged a couple of short trips off the dispatch board afterwards, calling it a night at 10 PM. Not a good start.

After all these years in this business, I realize there will be good days and bad. I have also inhabited this planet long enough to know nothing good lasts forever. While *ubering* the past few weeks, it was impossible to ignore the motionless gray cars adorned with *Z's* and lit-up hats, lining up three and four- deep at hotel taxi queues while I reaped ping after ping on my Uber phone. At times, I rolled up to hotels on cold and rainy nights, curiously quizzing my riders, "why wait for Uber when there are cabs in front of you ready to go?"

The answers ranged from general cab driver hatred to *we are used to Uber now*, to even in this enlightened era, *we didn't want to ride with a foreigner.* One day, as I pulled up to the Uber pick up area at the airport, as I loaded my passenger's bags, he asked, "no offense, but why don't they have taxis at this airport anymore?"

Somewhat astonished, I pointed to the four idle taxis parked twenty feet behind my car. "There *are* cabs...right there!"

He had noticed the name and lack of yellow distinction, and thought they were in fact *Zip Cars*, the popular hourly rental car sharing company. My astonishment dissipated.
After my miserable Monday night, I had the entire day Tuesday to make up ground. Following a night of short, broken sleep, it was back in the saddle at 6:30 AM.

Two days before Thanksgiving should be easy money with everyone getting ready to high- tail it out of town. I could run some trips to the Greyhound or Mega Bus, catch a 'port or two. Yes, I knew 95% of everyone preferred Uber, Lyft, Super- Shuttle—anything except a cab. No worry, there was still that leftover 5% or so—I hoped.

I headed towards Squirrel Hill, confident of a good trip dropping into my lap. I checked the screen; again, empty taxis sitting here, there, and everywhere. Just a little dead spell, the calm before a storm. I settled into a parking space in the business district, prepared to chase any call within range. The app offered nothing. In the first hour, only three trips opened. I tried for all, but they were gone in a millisecond. So... I sat. And sat. Stared in disbelief at an empty screen. I even checked the Uber app. It seemed quiet; surely, they were busier than us, but no one was getting rich, there were only small, infrequent surges. In better times, a fraction of the cab fleet competently handled the Thanksgiving exodus. With the addition of several thousand Uber sheep to the flock, there was no longer enough to go around.

Two hours creeped by, almost 9AM, still without an icebreaker. Beyond frustrated, as I drifted slowly towards the university area, a Squirrel Hill call finally came my way.

It was not an airport trip, not even one to the bus station. It was not even a little old lady visiting her hairdresser. It was a contract trip at Taylor Allderdice High School, my alma mater, to transport a "sick child" home, paid courtesy of the Board of Education.

I seldom worked on weekday mornings, so this was my first such trip in years. My initial thought was, "Gee, I hope he doesn't puke in the car," but I recalled that this being the last day before Thanksgiving break for public schools, maybe he was just seeking a jump start on his vacation.

The sick child, a tall Black kid in his early teens, scampered towards the taxi, not looking particularly ill. The destination on the app was Park Hill Drive, in the East Hills, a crime-ridden, sixties housing project designed with the best of intentions while yielding the worst of results. The address was his aunt's place, who was at work, and he had no key.

Naturally, I eavesdropped his cell phone conversation. The early departure from school seemed more related to a "business venture" than anything requiring professional attention from the school nurse. I asked whether there was another place I could drop him off, as it was an especially frigid morning. He admitted to residing in Penn Hills, a suburb unaffiliated with Pittsburgh's school district, but using the East Hills address to "get a better education in the city."

None of this came as a shock. Upon reaching his destination, he explained how he needed to wait two hours for his "boy" to show up. I wished him a nice Thanksgiving and drove away, satisfied to contribute to someone's tax dollars in action. Nonetheless, after three frustrating hours on this bitterly frosty morning, all I had under my belt was a $19 taxi voucher!

My bad day escalated. By 2 PM, all I had earned between Monday night and Tuesday, was barely enough to cover my fuel and lease. I spied again on Uber's app, which displayed sporadic, yet moderate surges, while the taxi app remained in a virtual coma. At 2:15, I finally landed a decent trip. It was from a Shadyside mansion on a private road, a sixty-something man going to Thornberry, a well-manicured conclave of upscale townhomes in the western suburbs. A few years earlier, this would have been one of a string of expected not so bad cab trips, but I found myself wondering the entire ride, "why me instead of Uber?" The meter stopped at $28, coming to $38 with the much- appreciated $10 cash tip. I not only thanked him for that but surprised myself by adding this: "Thank you for choosing *Zee-Zee-Tripp*."

I thought about taking a shot at the airport for one last trip but eradicated that idea and started towards the garage. The $38 I just pocketed was essentially my entire earnings for the 24-hour lease. After 24 years of a taxi career spread over a 40-year span, this was truly one of my all-time lows in terms of profit. As I neared the headquarters of *Zee-Zee-Tripp*, with my finger a microsecond away from the *Log Off* key, the computer offered another fare. With an hour left on my lease, why not?

The call was from a truck repair shop in the industrial neighborhood of Woods Run, one mile upriver from *Zee-Zee* headquarters. The shop was located one block caddy corner behind Port Authority's Manchester building, the same place I interviewed for my real job twenty years earlier. "Thank G-d for real jobs," I thought as I passed the building, again wondering about these pesky little ironies.

A weary looking man, about half my age, stood shivering on the corner with his luggage. He opted for the shotgun seat, which was fine by me, as it had been a lonely 24 hours. It turned out he had a similarly sucky day at work as well. He was deadheading from Philly to his home in Iowa when his engine decided to become the big engine that quit. Following a two-hour ride in an oversized tow truck, he was in search of a not too expensive hotel not too far away. Had he used an Uber, he may have been greeted with a blank stare, or a "maybe *Siri* would know." This seasoned cabbie knew exactly what to do. We set sail towards Banksville Road, where Comfort and Days Inns neighbor one another.

I received a sincere thank you for the prompt pick up. He expressed hope that his truck would be repaired in time to see his family for the holiday. He said he had been on the road for six years and was looking to make a change. I confided that, after four decades, I was beginning to feel the same way. As we spilt from the outer end of the Fort Pitt Tunnels, without any forethought, I looked him in the eye and said, "I think you could be my final trip as a cabby. Ever."

He looked slightly stunned, but I sensed an understanding in his expression. As I opened the hatch of the SUV, and handed him his bag, he reciprocated with a twenty, saying "that's all you." A firm handshake and a shared holiday well wish felt like one of those rare moments of sincerity and mutual empathy. It was time to log off, put it in gear, and return to the garage.

During the short drive back, I wrestled with my thoughts. Was this *it*? Was that the final trip? My last day? The end of a prolonged era? There were no clear answers.

After parking the cab, I cashed out. Thanks to my last two trips, I barely eked out a $60 profit after seventeen grueling hours inside a gray Santa Fe. John, a cashier from the new regime, was in the cage. I threw him a fin, wished him a good one, and headed out the door.

The taxi yard was jammed full of empty gray cars and vans, with random specks of dull yellow sprinkled about. Some were caked with stale snow, while others desperately begged for a bath. I took a couple of steps, pulled the hoody over my head, and shivered silently outside the office door, absorbing the biting winds of change, pondering my next step. Was I finished? Is there any hope at all for the taxicab business?

I shut my eyes, recalling better days. Long trips. Sweet tips. Racing to the airport for one last late fare. Close calls. Scary moments. This all felt so far away, so long ago, but I will never forget any of it. No regrets.

I took a few more steps, stopped and leaned against an ancient yellow Crown Victoria parked next to the gate. I again closed my eyes, trying to imagine the first formerly yellow cab transitioning to gray. My mind flashed back. Way back. To this day, I never understood how I contracted a nasty strain of hepatitis at age seven. There were ten endless days in Children's Hospital, countless IVs stuck into my skinny arms. I barely weighed forty pounds and will never forget the ghostly yellow color of my skin— even my eyes. Dr. Saul, he called it jaundice. I felt it was time to die. I survived. In fact, I vividly remember upon finally being released, the ride home to our Mellon Street apartment, in a big, old, yellow Checker taxicab. We were a million miles from rich, but I'm confident my mom tipped that driver.

I pushed away from the cab, walking slowly through the gate. Does that classic canary colored taxi fade into a jaundiced hue the moment they apply that first spray of gray paint, if only for a second? Is the entire cab business in a death spiral, here and across the country? For better or for worse, this business has reached Stage Four; that wait and see, *need morphine please!* phase of life. I hope I'm dead wrong. I pray for a miracle yet envision no cure.

My car awaits a block away, in front of the now defunct strip club at 1600 Pennsylvania Avenue—oh, these little ironies! I exhaled smoke clouds into crisp November air, staring one last time at the hundreds of taxicabs squeezed into the yard along Beaver Avenue. I pick up the pace, maintaining my gaze at the gaggle of gray cars under an even grayer sky.

I recall a sticky summer night from long ago, in a place I still vividly sense, standing on Centre Avenue after my inaugural shift on a crazy new job, staring at an endless parade of yellow Checker taxis straddling a fence. That was nearly forty years ago, a brutal first night. I made almost no money and was lucky to escape with my life. Yet, I knew that I was supposed to come back and do it again—and did exactly that.

I turn around, taking one last look. It has been a long, long road, but not a bad trip. Not a bad trip at all. I begin a slow jog towards my awaiting car. It really is time to go, but I feel this peculiar, unexpected, unsolicited moisture forming inside my left eye, now the other eye. It's got to be from that fuckin' wind.

The End

*Ford
Crown Vic.*

Epilogue
2023

It has been over six years since I walked away from Yellow Cab's reincarnation, Zee-Zee Tripp. I also retired from Port Authority after 24 years; thank you for the pension. They have since copycatted the cab company and "rebranded" as Pittsburgh Regional Transit. I have no more commitments to report to work, but the workaholic within endures.

I still dabble within the gig world. Not only with Uncle Uber, but with his tech-bros, Lyft, and Door Dash, often all three at once—my side things even come in threes. Do I love Uber? No. Miss the cab life? Yes. Will I ever go back? Never—I'm good; my work life is fine. Part time. *Very* part time. Three- or four-hour days, three- or four-day weeks. Sometimes more, oftentimes less. Whatever I feel like—a good place to be.

At least 80% of my workload involves driving people's overpriced food around while they stay home. Most of them leave notes in the apps to leave it on the porch, some request *no contact* deliveries. Faceless and impersonal. Pandemic residue?

But I can be a people person when the mood strikes; after all, I remain a cab driver at heart. I did not run a single rideshare trip for the first year and a half of The Covid Age, which led me to discovering food gopher-hood. Now I still run an Uber or Lyft passenger here or there, if only for old times' sake. But I am selective—a cherry picker. Most of the offered trips are economically unviable and I wear my sub-15% acceptance rates as a badge of honor.

When Uber invaded our market, it was an economic boom for their drivers. They earned 80% of the client's fare, excluding the extra fees. Booking fee. Airport fee. Trust and safety fee. That's rich! For an extra dollar, you can pay *us* so *we* can afford to let *you* trust *us*. Within a year, they lowered their rates in sync with the driver commission being reduced. And every few months, fare reductions. Again. And again. Rinse and repeat. The drivers were assured, "trust us; we know what we're doing, and you will make more money." Uh...yeah. Okay.

Fast forward to the present. Uber's algorithm charges the riders any price *they* want to and pays the driver as little as a race- to- the- bottom auction permits. Taxis in their heyday were rightfully highly regulated. Any change in fare structure was subject to scrutiny by the Public Utility Commission. When Uber and Lyft hijacked that industry, for some strange reason, the regulators *vamoosed*. Now, two people can stand on the same corner after an event, put identical destinations in their apps at the same exact moment, and be charged drastically different fares. And the drivers who accept these trips will receive unequal compensation. And as long as this practice continues unchecked and unchallenged, it will persevere.

And those Uber euphemisms? Drivers are no longer referred to as *Partners*—not that they were ever really involved in an actual business partnership. Remember *The Sharing Economy*? What happened to that song? Gig drivers work more and more for less and less. The so-called sharing business model devolved into a filtered trickle- down scheme. Ten years ago, the average taxi from downtown to the airport yielded $45-$50 for the driver. Uber and Lyft drivers now post screenshots on social media offering as little as $12 and $13 for the same ride in an inflationary landscape ten years later. And, no, the riders do not get a break most of the time. Yet, amazingly, there are rideshare drivers willing to accept these rides.

I haven't accepted a ride to The Promised Land in months, though I accidentally accepted a trip about a month recently. Lyft offered $20.10 to run John to the airport, a 30-mile, 36-minute trip according to the app. Five years ago, the same ride paid drivers at least $50. Rather than canceling, I remained idle for a few minutes until John called wondering about my whereabouts. I asked him what he was being charged for the trip…how about $64!? I told him how much they were paying me and that I was going to cancel, with no charge to his account. He offered to pay me $65.00 in cash, which most drivers would accept in a heartbeat. Hello Jitney! I politely declined because it violated *The Community Guidelines* (lol). I have on rare occasions played jitney for cash since my cabbing days, but only for my former cab regulars and people I knew well. Like Rain Man, I'm an excellent driver, but anything can happen anywhere at any time to anyone. I canceled, and John was very empathetic.

Despite my misgivings, I continue to uber on. I lovingly dub the three enterprises who work with me as *Goober, Grift, and Door Douche.* If you have read my 70,000-plus words of wisdom and mumbo-jumbo, I know I don't even have to tell you, but I will—don't forget to tip. Even the Uber driver.

This book is dedicated to every person who ever spent even a day behind the wheel of a cab or worked for a taxi company. This dedication extends to all taxi imitators, including but not limited to cab drivers wearing bad suits (limo drivers), jitney drivers, rideshare drivers, shuttle drivers, and I could never leave out bus drivers. Thank you for your services.

I thought about taking a limousine.
Or at least a fancy car
But I ended up taking a taxi,
'Cause that's how I got this far.

— From **Sequel**, *by Harry Chapin*

Afterword

2023

Through the too many miles
And the too little smiles
I still remember you.

— From **Taxi**, by Harry Chapin

First and foremost, thank you! For not only coming along for the ride, but for not bailing at the first traffic light. I hope you found your trip enjoyable, perhaps even enlightening. Or, at the very least, not a bad trip.

I'm confident that the spiral notebook industry experienced a healthy bump from my writing process. Every chapter I penned was outlined, written, reworked, compared, contrasted, and revised using multiple notebooks, often side-by-side. The challenge of recreating these experiences became engaging, almost therapeutic for me. The tough part was selecting which stories to highlight. Hundreds of thousands of miles and thousands of hours of human interaction contributed to ample deposits in my memory bank.

My goal was not to simply compile a "greatest hits album" of the wildest taxi tales, but to include enough of them to enliven the book. The most exciting encounters did not universally translate into the most personally impactful. For example, in *Pharmaceutical Sales,* I wished to show the dynamics of a typical round trip "drug run" and had more than a few to choose from. Most often, these rides mirror the trip portrayed in this chapter. The passengers are vague about their destination, the driver recognizes their intent, sets some parameters, acknowledges that their "business" is none of his, they return to the cab, and are on their way. Sure, I have encountered situations in that arena which evolved into unanticipated, even dangerous adventures, but my wish was to illustrate that most of these trips were common tales for cabbies with minimal attached drama.

Almost Famous, starring an obscure baseball player, fits a similar mode. Over time, I have encountered dozens of athletes who carried much higher profiles than the bottom of the bullpen pitcher featured in this chapter. I had completed an earlier draft of a trip with a future NFL Hall of Fame player and his cheerleader girlfriend engaged in a political debate. When he asked for my opinion—politics inside a cab is not the best idea—I allied with his pretty girlfriend, and we continued the lively discussion all the way to the airport. It was not an easy decision to make when circumstances dictated that there was room for only one of these two pieces. In the end, the brief ride with the baseball player made the final cut because it showcased the humanity we share with celebrities of all stripes.

Along with my primary intent to create written snapshots from my own Yellow Cab memories, there were three additional aspirations for this book. The first was to preserve the work culture and history of the taxicab industry while documenting its evolution over periods of time. I composed chapters like *The Checkered Past, Rick Shaw,* and *Radio Days* as deep dives inside Pittsburgh's cab universe of the seventies and eighties. With the rise of the gig economy, it was foreseeable for the taxicab to join some inanimate version of an endangered species list. While I doubt cabs will ever become obsolete, the taxi business will never regain the viable and visible impact upon the urban landscapes it once dominated.

The second thing I hoped to do was mitigate the inaccurate and unfair perceptions people held towards cabbies. Sure, I acknowledge there are few professions held in lesser esteem. Cabbies have long been maligned and misunderstood. Add in the stereotypes of cab drivers being uneducated lowlifes who "take people the long way" and the "it's okay to puke in a cab" mentality. I hope *Not a Bad Trip* at least modified these ideas and showed that cabbies are human; some even intelligent, or at least nice people.

And third, while I cast myself as the protagonist, the 'burgh and its people were the most important characters. If you learned more about our big, small town than you knew prior to reading this book, I think I did my job. And, if you now include the word *Yinz* on your roster of favorite pronouns—mission accomplished!

Acknowledgements

A book's creation is so much more than a one-person show. Differing viewpoints and fresh sets of eyes are the writer's most effective prescriptions, something I never realized until embarking on this project.

I would like to thank my friends for their continued encouragement and patience over the years-long (my fault) process of completing this book. And thanks to all my *Beta* readers, including friends and colleagues at Port Authority, a few select cab—and even Uber passengers, for sampling and offering feedback on some early chapter drafts.

This book would not exist without the help, advice, and education attained by participating in writer's groups. Thanks to The Monroeville Penn-Writers for their support during the embryonic stages of my writing, and especially to The Bridgeville Writers for their invaluable critique and advice over the past few years. And for turning me into a better writer by sharing your talented work. I could never have become a master of the *M-dash* without Yinz.

To Tom, Francine, Jason, and the folks at Word Association Publishers, thanks for your patience and help bringing *Not a Bad Trip* into the literary world. And special thanks to forever friends Gary Graff and Richard Schwartz for their professional advice and expertise along the way. This Bud—or Iron City—is for you!

And to Yellow Cab, Checker Motor Company, fellow cabbies, and the thousands of humans who plopped their butts in my back seat and expressed a destination; thank you so very much. And to *The Voice of Yellow Cab,* the radio dispatchers who I often shared rocky relationships with, my gratitude for the title. Some of my favorite memories of cab-life were listening to your all-night talk shows. And I would be remiss to not acknowledge Fred, Henry, Kenny, and the others locked inside a cage for reminding me to "keep coming back."

Of course, the best is saved for last. My parents, Max, and Ruth, my *Bubie,* Molly Goldberg, and my brother Ben—may their memories be a collective blessing—and my sister, Linda whose siblinghood (is that a word?) has always been my blessing. And love to my (grown up) children, Justin, Jenna, Brian, and Rachel, and to Chester, my adorable grandson, for tolerating my many quirks and general weirdness.

And most of all, my wife and love of my life, Chris. You deserve more credit than I do for the existence of this book. You were there more than once to block the kick when I was ready to punt the idea. Thank you for your patience and support throughout every step. Your honest feedback on every chapter meant the world to me. And for your incredible tolerance of and guidance through my technological ineptitude—there are no words!

About the Author

H oward (Howie) Ehrlichman, born in 1957, is a Pittsburgh lifer. A 1979 Penn State graduate, he resides in the eastern suburbs with his wife, Christina, a dog, and some cats. Chris and Howie are proud parents of four children.

Howie's taxi career began in 1977. In 1984, he took a twelve year "break" to operate a dynamic food store in an iconic Pittsburgh neighborhood. After selling his business, he returned to Yellow Cab in 1996. Two years later, he fulfilled his childhood dream, becoming a bus operator, and later, a dispatch-supervisor, retiring after

24 years. Throughout his transit career, he remained a dedicated weekend warrior at the cab company.

Not a Bad Trip is Howie's first book. He turned in his cab for the last time in 2016, ending his forty-year long love affair with taxicab life. Although officially retired, he still dabbles in the gig world of food delivery and rideshare.

WA